Other books by
Col Narinder Kumar

Nilakantha

•

Indus Boat Expedition

•

Trisul Ski Expedition
(co-author)

KANCHENJUNGA

KANCHE

Col Narinder Kumar, PVSM, AVSM

NJUNGA

First Ascent
from the North-East Spur

Vision Books

To Mridula
and
all Kanchenjunga wives,
especially Mrs Sukhvinder Singh.
Theirs were the highest stakes in the expedition.

First published in 1978

© The Adjutant General, Indian Army 1978

Published by
Vision Books Private Limited
36 C, Connaught Place, New Delhi 110001 India

Printed at
Thomson Press (India) Limited, Faridabad, India

Foreword

Mountaineering inculcates in a man courage, comradeship, the capacity to bear hardships and the ability to take deliberate decisions which may often entail consequences that may result in death. Those of us who have faced the imponderables of war know that young people, when suddenly confronted with serious situations, assume responsibilities and display great initiative and character which would otherwise lie dormant in them. One cannot ask for a war in order to foster leadership qualities. However, similar transformations frequently result from comparable experiences in peace when stimulated by the hazards of adventure sports such as mountaineering. This aspect of leadership apart, training in mountaineering techniques assumes a very important role in our Army, which remains deployed all along the Himalayas. The Army has, therefore, been able to produce a fine crop of mountaineers in India, not by mere chance alone.

In the glorious history of Indian mountaineering, the Army has always been in the fore and its representatives have acquitted themselves creditably. To mention a few, Major ND Jayal, a pioneer of mountaineering in India, Brigadier Gyan Singh, Leader of the first Everest Expedition (in which Colonel Narinder Kumar, PVSM, AVSM, took part as a Captain) led a summit team which failed to reach the Everest summit by a mere 700 feet; Major John Dias, Leader of the second Everest Expedition and Colonel Kumar himself the Deputy Leader of the third famous Everest Expedition, which put nine mountaineers on the top. Colonel Narinder Kumar, is one of the most experienced leaders of expeditions in the Himalayas today. He has led many a successful expedition to some of the highest mountains in Bhutan, Sikkim, Nepal, Central Himalayas and Kashmir Himalayas. This is in spite of the fact that he lost his toes during one of his many mountaineering adventures; and the doctors had declared that he must climb no more!

When great demands are made, greater response comes forth. I had, therefore, posed the most difficult challenge of climbing Kanchenjunga to Colonel Kumar and his team, because I had full faith in my men and the conviction that they can achieve anything, given an opportunity. They have more than lived up to my expectations. The conception, planning and execution of the ascent is an account of great courage, endurance and organisation by a team, of whose achievement we in the Indian Army can be proud.

The Army Expedition to Kanchenjunga, in flagrant defiance of many difficulties—a shortage of time, a paucity of equipment, vindictive terrain, treacherous weather conditions and the handicap of a tragedy which struck them early, nevertheless forged ahead. The story of Kanchenjunga Army Expedition, told with touches of humour, is inspiring and I hope the book will be widely read, particularly by our youth.

(T.N. Raina)
General

3 May 78

Contents

Colour Plates

Black and White Plates

Maps and Sketches

Preface

After my return from the Neelkantha Expedition in 1961, I along with the other members of the team called on Pandit Jawaharlal Nehru, the late Prime Minister of India. Panditji spent half-an-hour with us, intently listening to the story of our expedition. When we were about to leave, he said to me, "I hope you will write about your experiences." Though I said 'yes' then to Panditji, my true feeling was that I would rather climb the mountain again, than write a book, for as an expressly outdoor man I have never been very keen on the three R's. However, as it later turned out, I did manage to write the book and proved Johnson's words, "Any blockhead can write a book if he sets himself to do it."

In retrospect, I am happy I wrote it. I am not sure how many people have read that account. But I have relived my Neelkantha adventure many a time by glancing through it.

But the present book was planned even before we left for Kanchenjunga. It was partly with a view to finding some finances to meet some part of the huge expenditure being incurred by us on the expedition. Partly it was to provide a faithful record of the virgin routes we were going to traverse on this toughest mountain of the world. For without regard to, our success or failure in the attempt, its account would prove useful to whoever follows us later.

Kanchenjunga had ever been my dream mountain since the first day I became interested in mountains. And I had always cherished a strong desire in me to climb it.

Possessed by the idea, I was all the time planning Kanchenjunga expedition in my mind and thinking out methods of overcoming the problems faced by the earlier German expedition. My opportunity came when I met General T.N. Raina, MVC, and proposed such an expedition to him. The General, who knew me well from our long regimental association, put implicit faith in me and approved the idea. But to those who could objectively and dispassionately look at the proposal it was a foolhardy idea, fraught with risks and doubtlessly doomed to fail. That this view was held by the highest mountaineering circles in India, did nothing much to reassure me. However, General Raina's confidence in me was fully shared by the present Vice-Chief Lt-General O.P. Malhotra, PVSM, the then Vice-Chief Lt-General A.M. Vohra, PVSM, and Maj-General S.C. Sinha, the Director Military Training.

It was basically this grand confidence in me which encouraged and inspired me and other members of my team to fight against and overcome heavy odds.

11

In fact, the expedition continuously faced all sorts of troubles. We encountered the roughest weather known in the last 200 years, avalanches, rock falls, snow blizzards, high altitude sickness, even death struck one of our team mates.

In an expedition of this magnitude it is always the team work which is important; as no effort, howsoever big, can bring results unless it is well coordinated and correlated. On mountain heights, it is never the question of equal sharing; but it is the question of giving the maximum and accepting the minimum, with gratitude. This was the spirit which our boys showed throughout. The expedition has undoubtedly proved that it is not necessarily the stalwarts who make a big expedition successful, but it is the discipline and the concerted team effort which is the keynote of success.

Therefore I would like to express my deep gratitude and admiration of the members of my team, the Sherpas and the Ladakh Scout boys who worked in a spirit of perfect cooperation with each other, to make the expedition a success. Many of us shall remember with great appreciation the training we had been imparted at the High Altitude Warfare School of the Army.

Indian Air Force helped our expedition out of many tight corners, specially in evacuating the casualties.

My grateful thanks are due to Lt-General O.P. Malhotra, PVSM, Lt-General A.M. Vohra, PVSM, GOC-in-C, Southern Command, Lt-General J.F.R. Jacob, PVSM, GOC-in-C, Eastern Command, Lt-General W.A.G. Pinto, PVSM, Lt-General A.N. Mathur, PVSM, Lt-General Kundan Singh, PVSM, Lt-General Gurbachan Singh, PVSM, Maj-General S.C. Sinha, Maj-General M.C.S. Menon, AVSM, Maj-General A.K. Bhattacharya, AVSM, VSM, Brigadier T.G. Verma, Lt-Colonel D.N. Tankha, AVSM, Major S. Mahindroo, Major N.R. Naidu and Capt Jaspal Singh and scores of other officers who gave valuable help during the planning, preparation and conduct of the expedition deserve a special mention.

The space here does not permit me to individually list the names of all the persons who helped us in many ways. One of them, Mr H.C. Sarin, who made available to us his valuable experience in selecting the team deserves our thanks. Our thanks are also due to Indian Mountaineering Foundation for loaning us some mountaineering equipment and Himalayan Mountaineering Institute, Darjeeling, for offering us training facilities.

For the book to have become possible my grateful thanks are due to Lt-General E.A. Vas, PVSM, Brigadier Teg Bahadur Kapur, AVSM, and Lt-Colonel Bhisham Kumar, VSM, who took upon themselves the entire project.

Last but not the least I would like to thank Shri Kapil Malhotra, Director, and Shri Krishna Kumar, Managing Editor, Vision Books, for helping me with the script and selection of pictures for the book.   **NK**

FACING: (Above) *Kanchenjunga, an aerial view from the south.* (Below) *General T.N. Raina, MVC, Chief of the Army Staff, gives the green signal to Colonel Kumar to organize an Indian Army Expedition to Kanchenjunga.*

1

The Vision

The Idea Is Born

I was only twelve when I attended a Boy Scouts' Camp at Tara Devi in the hill state of Himachal Pradesh. I was immensely moved by the beauty around me: the pine trees, the heady scent, the cool breeze coursing through the glistening brown needles: it was a wonderful world. At night we slept pressed close to the earth inside a tent, while outside the rain played its soft symphony all about us. A new awareness was taking seed in me. I was being introduced to the mystique of the mountains.

Years passed. I was commissioned into the Kumaon Regiment of the Indian Army. Posted at the hill station of Ranikhet I had my first glimpse of the Himalayas. The sight left me awestruck and filled me with an unknown yearning. Then one day I read in a newspaper that Major Nandu Jayal was attempting to climb Nanda Devi, at that time the highest mountain in India. From Ranikhet, Nanda Devi appears as the centrepiece of the Central Himalayas. Filled with an uncontrollable desire to watch the assault, I set myself up with a powerful telescope trained at the mountain. In my enthusiasm, I spent hours scanning the peak but saw nothing of the expedition. My eyes smarted with the strain but I remained glued to the instrument. I longed to be up there on the snows and felt that destiny had somehow

FACING: *Kanchenjunga from the east.*

gone astray. A month later I was still looking at the mountain when I was told that the expedition had been called off weeks earlier.

A year later, in 1958, I was sent to learn basic mountaineering at the Himalayan Mountaineering Institute, Darjeeling, and first set my eyes on Kanchenjunga. Early in the training programme we were taken to Tiger Hill which also offers a view of Mt Everest. Everest, I must confess, was rather disappointing. It was completely dwarfed by the majestic Kanchenjunga. I saw green hills rising from the river Rangit, then a layer of blue haze, and jutting through the mists the Kanchenjunga massif clad in pure white snow. The fascinating view hypnotized me and was indelibly stamped on my mind. After our training in Darjeeling, we were told we were heading towards Kanchenjunga for a few days in the field. In childlike excitement, I asked Tenzing Norgay, Director of Field Training, "Shall we climb Kanchenjunga?" He had a hearty laugh at this, leaving me chastened and feeling an amateur.

A lot happened between then and 1966, when I was posted as the Principal of the same institute at Darjeeling. We had scaled Nanda Devi and Everest; I had lost my toes on Neelkantha and had almost to relearn walking. However, the desire to attempt Kanchenjunga remained unfulfilled. I had just to look through my bedroom window to see it shining like molten gold in the rising sun. Pink and crimson clouds with a golden lining adorned its proud bosom like a garland of wild flowers. My fascination grew so great that I changed my room for another, which offered a better view of the massif. Unable to restrain myself after a while, I requested for an audience with the Chogyal, the then Maharaja of Sikkim, to seek his approval for an expedition to Kanchenjunga.

Palden Thondup Namgyal, the Chogyal of Sikkim, was an impeccable host. My first day with him was spent in a round of festivities. When we met again the next day we first discussed some minor points regarding the building of mountain huts for field training in Western Sikkim. Seeing both the Chogyal and his wife Gyalmo pleased and in a happy mood I made my proposal. But nothing came of it and I felt destiny had once again conspired against me.

Years later, with a political realignment, Sikkim merged with India. Power was transferred from the Chogyal to the elected representatives of the people, and my heart beat again with a faint hope.

In 1976, I had led a Trisul Ski Expedition. On the successful completion of this adventure, I had the opportunity to meet General T.N. Raina, MVC, the Chief of the Army Staff, at an informal dinner hosted in his honour at Joshimath. I was pleasantly surprised by the General's interest in our expedition and he had obviously been following it very keenly. During the course of our conversation he remarked, "Half of our Army is deployed at high altitudes. Why can't we organize some big mountaineering expedition?" He also observed that most of the major Indian mountaineering expeditions had included Army personnel as leaders and members. The first and the second Indian Everest expeditions had been led by Army officers. In the third successful expedition to Everest, half the climbers had been from the Army. Army officers had also led expeditions to Nanda Devi, Chomalhari and Changabang. There was indeed a case for a major Army expedition, perhaps one without precedence in its projected goals.

"We should try Kanchenjunga from the east," I said. "It is perhaps the biggest prize left for mountaineers in the world."

To my great joy the General was very enthusiastic about the proposal. And all at once that was the only thing that seemed important. I left my job as Principal of the Indian Institute of Skiing and Mountaineering, and concentrated solely upon directing my energies at organizing an expedition to Kanchenjunga.

But my dream was not going to be realized quite so easily, and we were to face many harrowing pre-expedition ordeals. A few weeks after the initial announcement of the expedition, our venture started attracting a rather cold and hostile response. Mountaineering experts in India were convinced that the route I had selected was impossible, in any case, for the Indians who, they felt, were not ready for such an ambitious expedition. The Chairman of the Indian Mountaineering Foundation wrote a letter to the Chief of Army Staff advising him to carry out only a reconnaissance rather than launch a major expedition. The Chief, after consultation with the then Vice-Chief, Lt-General A.M. Vohra, PVSM, and Maj-General S.C. Sinha, Director of Military Training, however, supported the idea of a full scale expedition up the 'impossible' route. With this wonderful gesture, the Army demonstrated that it fully backed my judgement.

My heart now beat wildly. I was finally on the trail of the elusive Kanchenjunga.

Bhotia children of Lachen.

2

Five Treasures
of the Snow

With a confirmed height of 28,208 feet (8,598 metres) above sea level, Kanchenjunga is the third highest mountain in the world. The difference in height between Kanchenjunga and the second highest mountain of the world K 2, which rises to 28,253 feet (8,611 metres), is so little that Lord John Hunt had observed, "Its height alone makes it the third, and perhaps even the second highest mountain in the world."

Spelt earlier as Kangchenjunga by Kenneth Mason and others, it has also often been written as Kangchendzonga, a version obviously derived from the monastic circles. Among the Sikkimese and the people of the surrounding regions, the Kangchendzonga Deity is greatly revered along with numerous manifestations of Buddha. Kanchenjunga literally means 'five treasures of the snow', which are represented by: salt, crops, holy books, gold or turquoise and weapons. Kanchenjunga is thus a mountain to be looked upon with great veneration. The inhabitants of the surrounding valleys believe that the top of Kanchenjunga houses an all-powerful god, who guides their destinies and rules their fates. Their lives, their crops, indeed their very moods depend upon his benevolence; for when angry, the god destroys their villages by avalanches and floods. From the gravest disorder to a common illness, all are attributed to the wrath of this powerful deity. In their effort to placate this unpredictable god, lamas attired in ceremonial dresses and masks dance furiously for weeks. The dances, now known as the Kanchenjunga Dances, are held prior to the harvest, and are aimed at

18

pleasing this god.

Little wonder then that the lamas were scandalized by the news of our attempt to climb this mountain. On hearing of our expedition, one of the lamas issued the following statement which appeared on the front page of a premier English daily, *The Times of India*:

Kanchenjunga Angry

By Our Correspondent

GANGTOK, March 31: Monastic circles here have reported an unusual phenomenon associated with Kanchenjunga. Lama Karma Gyampo, MLA, who belongs to the old Rumtek Monastery, said here yesterday that he received a report of a big explosion heard from the direction of Kanchenjunga on March 27. It was followed by heavy landslides, perhaps avalanches, the next day. The Lama said the phenomenon had affected the nearby Tongshiong Glacier.

According to monastic circles, such an incident had never occurred in living memory. Scores of coolies engaged in road construction works near the Green Lake had suddenly fallen sick.

Reports from Mangan said that tens of thousands of dead fish had been sweeping down the Rakhel Chu and Talaung Chu rivers to Sangkhalang during the past two days. The Rakhel Chu originates from the Tongshiong Glacier.

According to Lama Karma Gyampo, it is considered by the local people as a manifestation of the wrath of gods, at the attempts being made by an expedition to scale the mountain which is the protecting deity of Sikkim, and hence sacred. Prayers are being offered at Lachung Gompa to avert ominous portents.

The people of Sikkim are not alone in their worship of the mountains. Indeed, earlier naturist religions have accorded an important place to mountain gods in their pantheons. When I had led an expedition to Nanda Devi in 1964, the locals believed that it was impossible to climb the 'Sacred Goddess'. I pointed out that Bill Tilman had done it before and that ours was to be the second ascent. They nodded their heads but kept insisting, "No one can do it, no one." There is a Nanda Devi Temple in a village called Lata, where one must pray and pay one's obeisance to the goddess. Our prayers were answered and the expedition was successful, but the locals just did not accept our claim.

Later, in 1970, I had successfully led an expedition to Chomalhari, setting up an altitude record in the Bhutan Himalayas. Chomalhari is the second highest peak in Bhutan, a mountainous country north-east of India. Everyone except His Majesty Druk Gyalpo Jigme Dorje Wangchuk, the King of Bhutan, who sponsored the expedition, had gloomy forecasts for us. "Even if you climb the

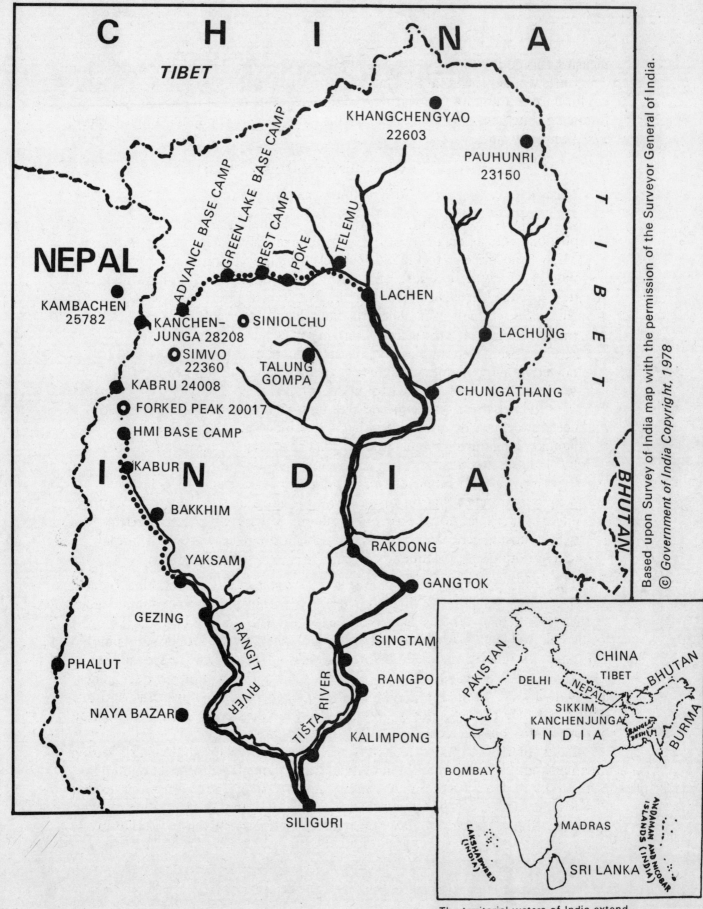

CHINA

TIBET

KHANGCHENGYAO
22603

PAUHUNRI
23150

NEPAL

KAMBACHEN
25782

ADVANCE BASE CAMP

GREEN LAKE BASE CAMP

REST CAMP

POKE

TELEMU

KANCHEN-
JUNGA 28208

SINIOLCHU

SIMVO
22360

KABRU 24008

FORKED PEAK 20017

HMI BASE CAMP

TALUNG
GOMPA

LACHEN

LACHUNG

CHUNGATHANG

KABUR

BAKKHIM

YAKSAM

GEZING

PHALUT

NAYA BAZAR

RAKDONG

GANGTOK

SINGTAM

RANGPO

KALIMPONG

RANGIT RIVER

TIŠTA RIVER

SILIGURI

BHUTAN

Based upon Survey of India map with the permission of the Surveyor General of India.
© *Government of India Copyright, 1978*

PAKISTAN

DELHI

CHINA

TIBET

NEPAL

BHUTAN

SIKKIM

KANCHENJUNGA

I N D I A

BURMA

BOMBAY

BANGLA DESH

LAKSHADWEEP (INDIA)

MADRAS

ANDAMAN AND NICOBAR ISLANDS (INDIA)

SRI LANKA

The territorial waters of India extend
into the sea to a distance of twelve nautical
miles measured from the appropriate base line

peak, Chomalhari goddess will never allow you to return," we were warned. Two Bhutanese who had been trained to go with us, withdrew at the eleventh hour after intense browbeating by the priests and we had to replace them with complete novices. Selected at the last moment, the new men escaped the influence of the prevailing pessimism but when one of them was only 50 feet from the summit, he refused to go on and desecrate his goddess. We climbed the peak but respected his sentiments.

The original inhabitants of Sikkim are the Lepchas. They have also been referred to as the 'Rong-pa', the ravine folk. They are supposed to have migrated to this area from the Assam Hills in the early thirteenth century. Short in stature, they have a muscular physique but small hands and slender wrists. They have mongoloid features, are beardless and slit-eyed and have a peaceful disposition. Initially spirit-worshippers, they also practised witchcraft and sorcery. The spirits of every stream, pass and hillock were appeased by offerings of stone, cloth

The packing assembly-line at Delhi.

or grain. Now most of these people have adopted Buddhism and are very devoted in their beliefs. They believe in the prophetic and symbolic nature of dreams. Thus, dreams showing them gathering wood or sand, for instance, or looking at a woman with a goitre, are held to be indicative of a good forthcoming harvest. Dreams of drinking foretell rain, and so on.

The second group of inhabitants in Sikkim are the Bhotias. Originally Khampas from Tibet, they have Tartar features with high cheek bones. Physically strong, they are boisterous in nature, as evidenced by our porters from Lachen. Their religion is Lamaism, and accordingly they have a Tibetan culture and dialect. However, these groups form only a quarter of the total population. The majority are of Nepalese origin, are very industrious and occupy most of the high bureaucratic offices and also control the bulk of the business. They are Hindus and speak Nepali.

Though Guru Padma Sambhava (Guru Rimpoche) had brought Buddhism to Sikkim in the eighth century, it was only in the seventeenth century that lamaism became a major religion. The tale goes that Lhatsum Chhembo flew over Kanchenjunga and came to a place called Kabur, a small rocky feature in the Dsongri Alps of Sikkim, where he met his followers. This myth had earlier caused me, in my days as Principal of the Himalayan Mountaineering Institute, to take a more tedious route to avoid trampling holy ground. Lhatsum Chhembo was joined at Yoksum by two other lamas. Together they called themselves the 'three superior ones'. Chhembo said, "The prophecy of Guru Rimpoche has it that four noble brothers shall meet in Sikkim and arrange for its government. We are three and have come from north, west and south. It has been said that there is in the east a man named Phuntshong, a descendant of brave ancestors from Kham in Tibet. He is to be our fourth member." In accordance with the prophecy they searched for this last member, found him and made him king in 1642, with the title of 'Chogyal' *(Dharma-raja)*. Thereafter, the Bhotias from Tibet have ruled Sikkim, and lamaism has been the state religion.

Lamaism itself is divided into two schools; the Nyingmapa, founded by Guru Rimpoche, and an earlier branch of Kargupa formed by the great yogi Marpa. The Head Lama of this latter section, known as the Karmapa, never hesitates to give his blessings to mountaineers. My previous meeting with him, when I had been accompanied by an ace mountaineer Sonam Gyatso, had given me ample proof of that. Unfortunately, the great encouragement his blessings would have given me was denied this time, since the Karmapa was away visiting.

Geographically, Sikkim is bounded by Tibet in the north and north-east and Bhutan in the east. Nepal lies to the west and West Bengal creeps up from the

---

FACING: (Above) *The walking wealth of the North Sikkimese: A Yak grazing in the Sikkim Alps.* (Below left) *Bhotia belle who carried 25 kilograms of load on the approach march.* (Below right) *A traditional lama dance.*

22

south. Sikkim thus forms a gigantic mountainous amphitheatre sloping towards the plains. While all the Himalayan mountains have an individual aura of their own, as also a great range of weather, Kanchenjunga is unique, as Frank Smythe points out, in that it is an independent mountain with its own glacier systems and its own weather. Contrary to general belief, Kanchenjunga does not lie on the Great Himalayan Range which is about 12 kilometres north of it. This range marks a giant watershed between the arid Tibetan Plateau on the north, and Sikkim in the south. Kanchenjunga acts as a protective bastion to the Great Himalayan Range, shielding it from the onslaught of the south-east monsoons which originate from the Bay of Bengal. Consequently, the annual precipitation of snow on Kanchenjunga is perhaps much greater than on any other mountain in the Himalayas. Due to the heavy snowfall, the faces and contours of Kanchenjunga are plastered with snow and ice, forming numerous hanging glaciers that move downwards to meet the main glaciers. The sheer faces of Kanchenjunga ensure that these huge masses of ice do not remain attached to them for long, and big boulders of ice regularly fall off. Bouncing and rolling over thousands of feet, these blocks polish the faces of the mountain till they shine like burnished metal. These avalanches comprise the deadly arsenal of Kanchenjunga. Some of the slopes are so sheer that the snow has no time to harden into ice, and rolls down as soon as it accumulates to a depth of about six inches. Such slopes are extremely dangerous for climbers.

Some parts on the eastern side, where the slope is not very steep, are packed with snow which is driven on to the slopes by the strong westerly winds, creating invariably dangerous windslabs. Frank Smythe wrote, "There is probably no other mountain in the world where the mountaineer is exposed to greater dangers than he is on Kanchenjunga, for not only has he ice avalanches to contend with, but uncertain weather as well. Weather in Kanchenjunga is incalculable both in cause and effect."

Apart from being subjected to normal changes of weather, Kanchenjunga also creates its own climatic conditions. Once, there was no depression approaching from the west, and no monsoons in sight either, but we experienced a blizzard of such blinding intensity that it tore up our tents. After two long hours there was a sudden lull, the sky miraculously cleared and perfect calm descended on the mountain. One often finds a fine morning suddenly turning overcast and stormy for no apparent reason. Such unpredictable changes of weather make mountaineering efforts in the region very chancy. A self-respecting pundit would lose his following were he to try and earn his fortune by foretelling the weather conditions on Kanchenjunga!

FACING: *The floral wealth of the Sikkim Himalayas.*

3

The Previous Attempts

The panoramic view of Kanchenjunga from Darjeeling, a hill station 250 miles north of Calcutta, is one of the grandest in the world. Immediately beyond the town the ground falls away steeply to the bed of river Rangit, barely 1,500 feet above sea level. North of Rangit, Sikkim stretches for the next 40 miles, "a crumpled world of forested ridges and deep tropical canyons." Further on, stately, tall brown alps and glistening ice-walls, culminate in the 5-mile high Kanchenjunga massif; its steep, fluted white walls harbouring ice, snow and avalanches. To a mountaineer's eye, Kanchenjunga looks an impregnable giant even from this distance. Situated in such spectacular setting, it has long worked its lure on mountaineers from all parts of the world.

Climbers had started knocking at the southern portals of Kanchenjunga even before Everest was discovered in 1852 to be the highest mountain in the world. Sir Joseph Dalton Hooker was the first foreigner to explore this region with a botanical expedition. While in the area, Sir Hooker and Dr Campbell were seized and imprisoned by the order of the Dewan (Prime Minister) of Sikkim. Thereupon, the British sent a punitive expedition and established their control on the foreign affairs of Sikkim, opening the area for subsequent explorations. Sir Joseph Hooker had thus unknowingly triggered an action which changed the course of history. Who knows, but for him Kanchenjunga might still have been unclimbed from the east!

In 1883, W.W. Graham led the first mountaineering expedition to the

Kanchenjunga massif and claimed to have climbed the 24,002-foot (7,316 metres) Kabru from the south-east. As this was a world altitude record at that time, much controversy ensued. Graham's claim remains in doubt to this day. Many people think that he had mistaken Forked Peak for Kabru. But even if he had climbed Forked Peak it was a great achievement. Having visited the base of Forked Peak nearly two dozen times myself, I can vouch that it is not an easy peak to climb. In 1879, Babu Sarat Chandra Das, one of the renowned Pundits (Indian surveyors were called by this term at that time) made a bold journey to this area and crossed the 20,080-foot (6,120 metres) high Jonsongla; a great feat indeed.

The backbone of the Kanchenjunga massif is the North-South Ridge with the main summit as its highest point. The second highest peak of the massif, known as the South Summit, is also located on this ridge, one kilometre south of the main summit. At 27,808 feet (8,476 metres), this is the highest unclimbed mountain in the world at the moment. The other main peaks on the ridge are Simvo and Siniolchu. The famous Zemu Gap also lies on this ridge. The West Ridge joins the North-South Ridge at its highest point, i.e. the main summit. Important peaks on the West Ridge are Kangbachen and Jannu.

The Eastern Ridge of Kanchenjunga meets with the North-South Ridge at the South Summit. The important peaks on this ridge are, the Twins Peak, the Nepal Peak, the Tent Peak, Talung, Kabru and Rathong. There are two notable features of this ridge. The first is the North Col, a depression which is the lowest part on the ridge between the main summit and the Twins Peak, and the other, an easterly offshoot known as the North-East Spur, even though it runs almost directly east. It is called the North-East Spur probably because, firstly, this Spur takes off from the North Ridge, and secondly, this name helps distinguish it from the main East Ridge.

The first serious reconnaissance of Kanchenjunga was carried out in 1899 by William Douglas Freshfield, who made a 7-week trip to assess the possible climbing routes. He made a thorough study and suggested that it may be possible to climb the mountain via the Kanchenjunga Glacier and the North Ridge. He also visited the Zemu Glacier, observed the North-East Spur, and wrote, "The right hand buttress is a marvel of mountain architecture: it springs from a low mass or pedestal of splintered granite, and flies up in an icy arete of a length and steepness which defy alpine comparison, until it rests against the Northern Ridge." His experienced eye saw no possibility of climbing the Spur. We intended to take this route.

In 1905, a small expedition consisting of three Swiss—Jacot-Guillarmod, Reymond and Lieut Pachi—an Italian, De Righi, and led by a Britisher, Aleister Crowley attempted the North-West Face from the Yalung Glacier. Crowley was somewhat of a self-centred eccentric, called himself 'The Great Beast of the Apocalypse', and practised black magic. He ill-treated the porters, failed to supply them with boots which he had promised, and asked them to walk barefoot

An aerial view of the various ridges and glaciers of the Kanchenjunga massif.

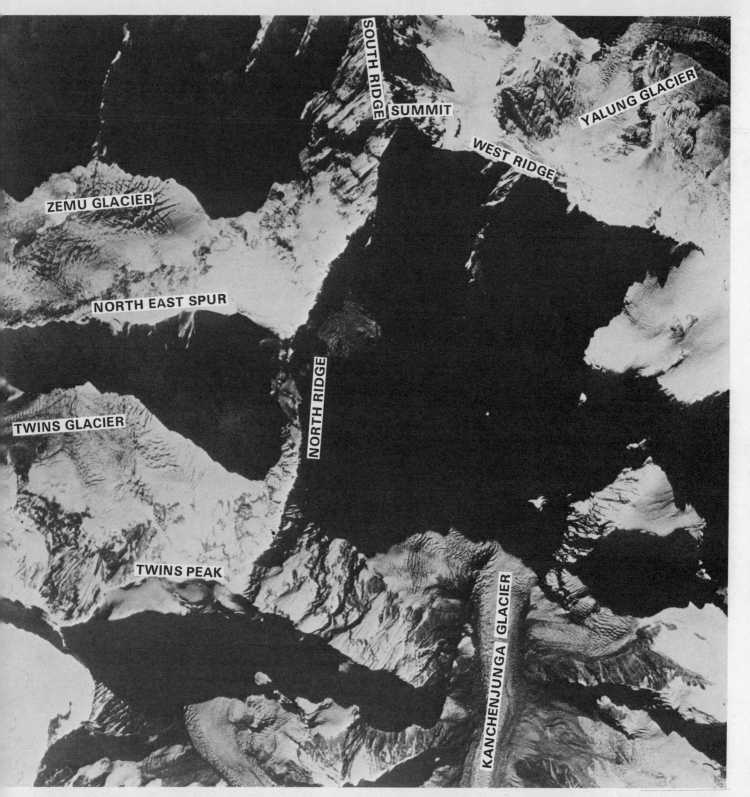

An aerial view of the North-East Spur and the North Ridge.

on snow by invoking supernatural powers. In growing discontent, the other members held a high-altitude conference, deposed Crowley as the leader, and called off the expedition. Everyone descended except Crowley and Reymond.

While descending, one of them slipped and started an avalanche. The entire rope of six climbers was caught in this avalanche and hurtled down. Only Guillarmod and De Righi survived. They started searching for Pachi and the three porters and shouted for help. Reymond came down from the camp to their aid but the deposed leader did not join the search efforts. The following day, all members and porters except Crowley went up again to dig for the bodies. Crowley was coming down at that time but did not stop. Deserting the team, he reached Darjeeling alone, living up to his nick-name 'The Great Beast'.

This tragedy sickened and horrified climbers all over the world, and Kanchenjunga was left alone for the next 25 years till an American, E.F. Farmer from New York, attempted a lone ascent from the Talung Glacier. He was accompanied by three experienced sherpas of Everest fame. Unfortunately, they did not have crampons, so he left them at the Base Camp and started climbing alone, turning a deaf ear to the dissuading pleas of his sherpas. The sherpas saw him climbing, a tiny speck moving on the vast snow slopes, until the mists enveloped him and he never returned. The curtain was thus rung down on the second tragedy on Kanchenjunga.

The two attempts had been so weak that Kanchenjunga had not been called upon to use its real weapons—avalanches, blizzards, precipices and rarefied air. Its complacency was however rudely shaken in the autumn of 1929. Paul Bauer with the pick of German climbers, perhaps the best in the world at that time, made an attempt from the steep, icy and saw-edged North-East Spur. Of course, Freshfield had earlier seen and described this Spur but it had looked so impossible to him that he had not even suggested this as one of the likely routes to the summit. For six weeks, the Germans fought grimly with the mountain. Defying the avalanches, they got to the crest of the Spur by crossing over sharp, serrated ribs of rock and fluted ice. But that was only the beginning of their problems. From there the Spur rose for thousands of feet, its crest a cock's-comb of unstable snow mushrooms and ice-embossed towers. When they got to an altitude of 22,500 feet, a heavy blizzard pinned them down for three days. They had no option but to return.

The descent was not easy either. They threw away their rucksacks while ploughing through man-deep troughs of fresh snow. The frost-bitten led the snow-blind down and it was a miracle that they came off the mountain without losing a life. Despite their failure the *British Alpine Journal* described their attempt as a "feat without parallel in all annals of mountaineering history". According to the publishers of the account, this expedition was awarded a Gold Medal at the Los Angeles Olympics. Requesting the Himalayan Club to help them Heliogolander Rickmers wrote before the expedition, "They want to test themselves

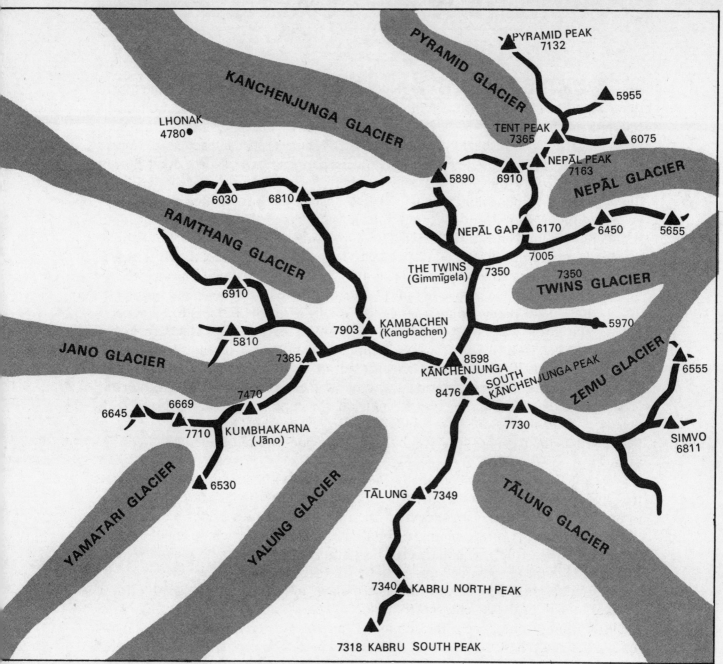

A map showing the various approaches to Kanchenjunga.

against something difficult, some mountain that will call out everything they have got in them, of courage, perseverance and endurance." And they had been certainly tested to the utmost.

In 1930, Prof G.O. Dyhrenfurth, who had an unequalled record of climbing 700 peaks in the Alps and Hohetara, took a team to Kanchenjunga. With him he had Marcel Kurz, a Swiss topographer, and the pace-setters in winter mountaineering, Heerlin and Schneider of Germany, who constituted the fastest climbing pair of Europe at that time and had made the first winter ascent of Blanche de Peuterey, one of the most dangerous climbs in the world, in less time than the summer ascent record. Frank Smythe was one of the British members. In all, there were five Germans, three British, two Swiss and one Austrian. Dyhrenfurth selected the North-West Face route from the Kanchenjunga Glacier. This had been suggested by Freshfield but not yet tried. They established their Base Camp in the upper basin of Kanchenjunga Glacier opposite the North-West Face. Their plan was to climb to the North Col that lies between the Twins Peak and the summit of Kanchenjunga, and then get on to the North Ridge. While they were making a route through an ice fall, a huge hanging glacier broke off and thundered down. The ensuing avalanche hurtled down towards a party of three members and 12 porters. They ran as fast as they could and luckily all escaped except Sherpa Chettan, the First Tiger of Everest. The expedition was abandoned after the reconnaissance of the West Ridge proved futile.

In 1931, Paul Bauer led another expedition of Munich climbers to Kanchenjunga. This team was larger and stronger than his earlier one. Once again he selected the North-East Spur for his attempt and came to the mountain six weeks earlier than in 1929. The expedition suffered an early setback. H. Schaller and two porters were moving up from the Eagle's Nest to the crest of the North-East Spur when Pasang, the second man on the rope, slipped and also pulled Schaller off the mountain, falling 1,700 feet to their deaths. Only the other porter was saved as the rope broke. After burying their bodies, Paul Bauer resumed the assault.

Again they were confronted by the ice towers, ice mushrooms and steep ice cliffs of the North-East Spur. Climbing from 21,800 to 22,800 feet, a mere thousand feet which can be covered in just a few hours under normal conditions, took them 13 days of tunnelling through ice towers and hacking away at the mushrooms. After mastering the North-East Spur, they came to a point from where they could see the face that led up to the North Ridge. Full of cracked wind-slabs, it appeared formidable due to avalanche danger and after careful scrutiny they decided to call off the expedition from 25,200 feet. It is heartbreaking to imagine them returning from so near the summit. If anyone deserved to climb Kanchenjunga, they did. These two German attempts were the forerunners to our eventual success on Kanchenjunga from this route.

In 1937, Lord John Hunt, Lady Hunt and C.R. Cooke made a plan to scale Peak 7780 on the Eastern Ridge of the Kanchenjunga massif. Upon reaching Darjeeling, however, they altered their plans and went to Zemu to reconnoitre the possibilities of climbing Kanchenjunga from its eastern flank. Lord Hunt got to the Zemu Gap, and Cooke also made a very daring attempt to reach the North Col.

FACING: (Above) *Our Yak caravan setting off from Lachen carrying the expedition loads.* (Below) *Siniolchu, the most beautiful mountain in the world.*
OVERLEAF: *Sunrise on Kanchenjunga.*

Sir John Hunt wrote after his successful Everest expedition of 1953, "There is no doubt, that those who first climb Kanchenjunga, will achieve the greatest feat of mountaineering for it is a mountain which combines in its defences not only severe handicaps of wind and weather and very high altitude, but technical climbing problems and objective dangers of an order higher than we found on Everest."

In 1953, John Kempe of the Hyderabad Public School took a close look at the South-West Face above the Yalung Glacier, the route taken by the ill-fated Crowley expedition 48 years earlier. He felt that if a way could be found to the great shelf above the Yalung Ice Fall, a strong team had a chance to reach the summit. To find this way, he led another reconnaissance expedition in 1954. The expedition probed up and down and finally found a way over the rocky rib on the right bank of the Ice Fall that took them half-way up this obstacle. Though this expedition did not reach very high, they had opened the route which was followed by the 1955 expedition led by Charles Evans. The Britishers succeeded in climbing Kanchenjunga from the North-West Face, the route suggested by John Kempe. Joe Brown and George Band reached the summit on May 25, followed by Tony Streather and Norman Hardie, the next day. But the mountain extracted its price. On their return they discovered that one of their sherpas had died of high altitude sickness.

The British team had doubtlessly done a great feat of mountaineering. But the route which had defied two great German expeditions, yet remained unconquered. It was this challenge we had accepted for ourselves.

FACING: (Above) *Telemu: the first stage of the approach march.* (Below) *The Rest Camp at 15,300 feet.*

Paul
Bauer

4

Siniolchu

Our Training Mountain

On October 6, 1976, I met the Chief of Army Staff in his office in New Delhi and was informed that our expedition had been cleared. I was overjoyed but also experienced anxiety about the state of our preparations since the time available was very short. It is one thing to conceive a big expedition but quite another to organize it efficiently. The expedition was placed under the Directorate of Military Training, then under the command of Lt-General W.A.G. Pinto, PVSM. As the first step, he immediately created a Kanchenjunga Cell, manned by Major N.R. Naidu and Major S. Mahindroo, who did an excellent job in helping me complete all preparations in time.

My first task was to select the team. I had been out of touch with the Army now for 11 years, and did not know many Army climbers. So I decided to hold a selection exercise. At first I thought of holding this in the Nun Kun region in Kashmir, but eventually settled for the 22,600-foot (6,880 metre) peak, Siniolchu on the East Ridge of the Kanchenjunga massif. I felt this would also perhaps give us a chance to reconnoitre the route we planned to take the following summer.

The climbers, who had been invited for selection, had already collected at Gangtok where I joined them on November 16, 1976. Gangtok, the capital city of Sikkim, situated on one of the spurs of the Chola range at a height of 5,500 feet, has a population of about 15,000. It is connected by a national highway to Siliguri in West Bengal, and is about 26 miles from the border town of Rangpo which is renowned for its liquors. Close to Gangtok is the famous monastery of Rumtek, an important seat of lamaism. Once only a village, Gangtok is now a modern town with its complex of secretariats constructed in typical Sikkimese style, an Institute of Tibetology, a Library of Tibetan Manuscripts and a Cottage Industries Institute. I had read in Freshfield's account of a monastery in Gangtok which depicted the Kanchenjunga deity as a "fearful, hungry spirit riding a white lion to whom the meat offerings must be made by the faithful". I have tried to locate this without success on numerous occasions. From the View Point, one gets a lovely view of a number of snowy peaks. Narsing is the nearest and very imposing. Kabru can be easily identified as is Pandim. Kanchenjunga stands as the undisputed monarch of the range. However, the view of Kanchenjunga from Gangtok is not at all the same as its view from Darjeeling. From here the peaks on the Kanchenjunga massif appear as separate mountains while from Darjeeling one can see the whole massif.

From Gangtok we motored to Chungathang. The road runs along the Teesta river most of the way and passes through some beautiful countryside. Despite the motorable highway the area is still unspoilt by the usual ugliness of urbanization. The forests are thick and unexplored and if one were to go only a few hundred yards inside them, one could easily get lost. There are pines, chestnut trees, rhododendrons, magnolia and hundreds of types of ferns and blooming orchids. No wonder Joseph Hooker had called Sikkim a paradise for the botanist.

On way to Chungathang, we passed through the famous view point, Singik. There is a lovely dak bungalow just above the road from where we had an unmatched view of sun-rise on Kanchenjunga. This dak bungalow is situated just above the confluence of the Lachen and Lachung streams. I had earlier been here in 1966 and had gone upto Zimithang hot springs in the Lachung valley but this time we were to follow the road to Lachen valley.

That evening, while out for a walk, I saw six of our Darjeeling sherpas hanging around with long faces. It turned out that they had not been allowed to dine in the Other Ranks Mess by the Havildar Quartermaster. The NCO was not to be blamed for he was only used to dealing with porters and did not know the special status sherpas enjoy. I explained this to the sherpas and took them back to the camp. Serious trouble was thus averted as they had decided to leave us and catch the next bus home.

Major J.K. Bajaj was our transport officer, perhaps the most efficient transport officer I have come across. With only 50 porters he managed to get us across to Siniolchu Base Camp, without wasting much time. On October 18, we reached Lachen, a village 16 miles from Chungathang. Lachen has a very spacious dak bungalow situated at a height of 9,000 feet, opposite the village across the road. On October 19, Joe (Lt-Colonel J.C. Joshi) and I started on the first stage of our approach march. Upto Zemu bridge the track was quite good. From there the normal route goes on to Giagong but we had to follow the closed valley of the Zemu Glacier.

In the Eastern Himalayas, one has invariably to cross thick forests to get to glaciers. But for the local porters, we would often have strayed from our track, which is narrow and thickly wooded with alpine flora. Rhododendron bushes grow in such abundance that they pose a stiff obstacle to the walker. They grow under the conifers and silver fir trees. The river bed near the Zemu bridge is wide and beautiful. Moss abounds on the rounded big boulders, lending a dash of colour to the otherwise predominantly green landscape. The track became badly broken after about 2 miles and often we had to climb the steep forest on the left bank of Zemu Chu (river) to avoid huge landslides. Our first stage was Telemu, just short of the confluence of Lhonak Chu and Zemu Chu. We selected a beautiful camping site carpeted with edelweiss.

The next day dawned clear. We had our first glimpse of the eastern face of Kanchenjunga and I spent an hour taking pictures. For approximately 8,000 feet, the mountain rose in sheer cliffs, plastered with hanging glaciers.

We crossed over the Lhonak Chu by a log bridge. The weather had turned chilly with a cold drizzle. After following the river bed for about half a mile, we stepped once again into the dark bowels of the jungle. We struggled through Himalayan larches and thick shrubs and rhododendron bushes. Having travelled for some time under the heavy foliage of the trees, we came upon a beautiful patch, thickly carpeted with velvety golden grass. It appeared a good camping spot, but I quickly changed my mind when I discovered that the golden grass covered swamp. Where the bog was deep, local people had placed thick planks and we had to perform various acrobatics to get across. At one place, both Joe and I leapt on to the same plank and to our horror it sank a full foot and the muck seeped into our boots, soaking our legs.

A little further we were surprised to come upon a small thatched hut. We had hardly expected to see signs of a settlement so much beyond Lachen. Pasang, one of our porters, explained that this was Yakthang, an important point on the old north-south trade route. The bridge over the Zemu Chu, a little beyond, connected this route between the Talung Monastery and Tibet. The bridge was strong enough to take fully loaded yaks, while earlier on in the Zemu valley, even people on foot had problems on the narrow track. Towards the south the track crosses the Yamtsola and goes on to the Talung Monastery and meets the North Sikkim Highway near Singik. It is believed that for the last 20 centuries, Talung Monastery used to house the valuables of all the monasteries in Western Sikkim, protecting them from roving brigands. Chief among these raiders were the Gurkha invaders. The key to the treasure room of the monastery at Talung, the story goes, was kept by the Chogyal at Gangtok. To the north, a track leads off towards Thangula and after Nakula crosses over into Tibet. The Sikkimese used to send timber to Tibet and bring salt from there through this route.

We walked a short distance along this historic route before returning to our camp. Taking off our socks to dry our feet, we felt happy to be underway.

Col Narinder Kumar

Major Prem Chand

Major S.S. Singh

Major Pushkar Chand

Capt K.I. Kumar

Capt Jai Bahuguna

Capt J. Cruz

Major S. Sen

Capt S. Cruz

Nb Sub Chering Norbu

Nb Sub Kura Ram

b Sub Gurcharan Singh

Nb Sub Nirmal Singh

Nb Sub Khushal Singh

Hav N.D. Sherpa

Naik P. Angchuk

Naik Dorje

Hav Jawahar Singh

The festive mood was contagious and all of us sat around the camp fire while the porters, including a large number of pretty female ones, danced and sang for us until late at night. An educated Bhotia interpreted the dances for us. The first one was a prayer to the deity of Kanchenjunga and another, performed by a couple of boys and girls, and as exquisite as the first, was a prayer to the Dalai Lama.

The next day saw us heading for our Siniolchu Base Camp, the site of the German Rest Camp in 1931. It was a level march through a maze of rhododendrons and birch. Two hours at a rapid pace got us to Yabuk. The forest ended here and hence onwards we encountered only sparse vegetation, the tallest of these being the 3-foot high rhododendrons, sheltering a carpet of edelweiss and large gentians. The next stretch took us down to the snout of the Zemu Glacier. A stream running parallel to the glacier in a depression between its left flank and the mountain cuts across and joins river Zemu Chu at this point. For an hour and a half we trudged on the lateral moraine before entering the meadow in the depression which took us through to the old German Rest Camp. And then suddenly, the curtain of mist that had concealed Kanchenjunga started lifting, and soon we had a clear view of Kanchenjunga's eastern flanks as also the Twins Peak and the Nepal Peak.

While our Base Camp was being set up, I took the other members of the selection committee, namely Lt-Colonel L.P. Sharma, Lt-Colonel J.C. Joshi and Major A.S. Cheema, to the top of the lateral moraine to have a look at Siniolchu, the peak we wanted to train on. I had known this mountain was beautiful but when we actually saw it, it took our breath away. It rose majestically like a sculptor's perfect model. Feasting on the glorious view, I outlined my plans for the ascent. I wanted to set up Camp I below the Ice Fall, which we could skirt from the right, and then climb to the Col between Siniolchu and Little Siniolchu. This latter portion would involve negotiating a broken glacier and crossing a ridge. We would need three camps: one below the Ice Fall, another above it and the third on the ridge itself. From where we now stood, only the last 200 feet to the summit seemed really difficult but I was not much worried by this, since getting to the summit was anyway secondary to our aim of choosing a team for the Kanchenjunga expedition.

We set up our Camp I on November 24, after crossing the Zemu Glacier and then making our way on to the Siniolchu Glacier itself. We had often to scramble over 100-foot mounds of rock and ice and skirt round the green ponds that dotted the surface of the glacier. There was one particularly frightening place on the Siniolchu glacier where stones, larger in size than a man's fist, incessantly tumbled down from obscure heights, creating a danger zone. We had to wait and try to figure out the pattern of the stone showers, and then rushed across during rare lulls. Imagine then my amazement on seeing a young local lad with two girls nonchalantly amble across this spot carrying heavy loads!

The support party of Ladakh Scouts

L/Nk Dharmanand   L/Nk Surinder Singh

High-altitude porters from Manali

Young Tenzing and Lepka Gyalbo

The Sherpas from Nepal

Ila Tshering   Hav Mutup

I had formed the climbers into different ropes to test their skills. As planned, the first party established Camp I above the Ice Fall at approximately 18,000 feet. The going was fairly good. Then we started our push to reach the ridge between Little Siniolchu and the main Siniolchu. My leave was coming to an end. But a lot of work yet remained unfinished and also new problems were cropping up. Some of the porters left us and went away to their homes to stock wood for the approaching winter months. Our brand new stoves did not work. The winter snows also hit us early. The Siniolchu Peak eluded us but our main purpose was served: we had had a chance to see the climbers at work. However, some known climbers had not been able to attend the selection camp. They were also eventually considered for final selection.

The final composition of our Kanchenjunga team was as follows:

I was to lead the expedition. Major Prem Chand was selected as the Deputy Leader. An ace mountaineer and the only man with the distinction of having climbed both the Nanda Devi Peaks, he had also made the ascent of the 23, 977-foot Chomalhari in Bhutan. Despite being a very devoted family man, Major Prem Chand seems to have dedicated his entire life to the mountains. He was also put in charge of our equipment.

Major S.S. Singh was the other Deputy Leader of the team. He had climbed Nun and skied down Trisul. Very tough but soft-spoken, he is an excellent companion in the mountains.

Next, we had the sprightly Capt K.I. Kumar who had been a valuable member of the Indo-American Nanda Devi expedition. He had lost an almost certain chance for the summit as a result of the fatal tragedy that overtook William Unsoeld's daughter Nanda Devi. He had also been on the Sasar Kangri expedition, the British Brahma expedition and had climbed Gankar South in Bhutan. On account of his being my brother, there were objections from certain quarters to Capt Kumar's inclusion, but his previous experience over-rode this factor and he went on to prove a great asset on the mountain.

Naik Nima Dorje Sherpa had tragically missed getting into the 1965 Everest team but had made the coveted first ascent of Sickle Moon, the highest peak in the Kishtwar Himalayas. He had also climbed Kamet, Bandar Punch, Trisul and Hogin III in the Garhwal Himalayas and virtually selected himself. Belonging to the Gurkha Regiment, he was to make a fine climbing pair with Major Prem Chand.

Next on the rolls was Havildar Norbu of Ladakh Scouts who climbs with the agility of a mountain goat and the strength of a yak. These qualities had helped him partner N.D. Sherpa in the first ascent of Sickle Moon. He had also climbed

FACING: *Simvo showing through mist.* OVERLEAF: (Above) *An early morning view from the Rest Camp.* (Below) *Our Base Camp at 16,200 feet.*

44

Umba Peak. Very obviously, he was a potential summiteer and lead climber for Kanchenjunga.

Then there was Company Hav-Major Gurcharan Singh who had scaled Kolahoi and Harmukh in Kashmir and skied down Trisul. He had been an instructor for three years at the High Altitude Warfare School.

We were fortunate in also having Company Hav-Major Nirmal Singh who had been a member of the Indo-American Nanda Devi expedition. A seasoned climber with numerous technically difficult climbs like Shivling to his credit, he was an instructor at the Nehru Institute of Mountaineering, Uttarkashi.

Company Hav-Major Kura Ram of the Kumaon Regiment had regularly climbed in Bhutan and had bagged four small but difficult peaks in Kashmir.

Havildar Sukhvindar Singh, while not very experienced in high altitude climbing, was the toughest of the lot.

Major Pushkar Chand of the Parachute Regiment had a couple of climbs in Kashmir to his credit and his speed on mountainous terrain was truly astonishing. He was put in charge of the porters on our approach march.

Havildar Jawahar Singh, our next member, had done a lot of climbing in the Poo Sector of Himachal Pradesh.

Captain Jude Lawrence Cruz was another Para Officer who had earned an enviable reputation at the mountaineering courses at the Nehru Institute of Mountaineering, Uttarkashi.

Naik Tashi Dorje of the Ladakh Scouts and Lance Naik Phunchok Angchuk fully lived up to the faith vested in them by the selection committee and proved invaluable to the team.

Captain Jai Bahuguna was a last-minute entry and was a promising mountaineer in the making. He had already climbed Jogin and is the brother of the renowned climber, late Harsha Bahuguna, who had died tragically during the International Everest expedition in 1970.

Our medical team consisted of the efficient Major S.S. Sen, who had earlier been on Nun and Capt S. Cruz, a newcomer to the mountains, but who did very well in the trial. We had S.R. Naidu of the Films Division to shoot a cine film of the expedition and Arun Dhar of Samachar, the national news agency, to provide press coverage. Lance-Naik Chandel and Lance-Naik Surinder Singh were our signal men.

The selected team was then sent to the Himalayan Mountaineering Institute at Darjeeling for refreshing their technical skills in preparation for the coming adventure. This training proved especially useful for the members from Ladakh Scouts, who knew little of advanced mountaineering techniques.

OVERLEAF: (Above) *An early morning view from the Rest Camp.* (Below) *The Zemu Gap.* FACING: *The lower portion of the Ice Fall. Some freshly fallen ice boulders can be seen near the climber.*

5

The Necessary Evil

Preparations

On December 8, my birthday, I left my job as the Principal of the Indian Institute of Skiing and Mountaineering in Gulmarg, and stationed myself in Delhi to complete our preparations for the expedition. We had only three months' time which I knew was desperately short to organize an expedition of this size. On the other hand, I felt that if the expedition were to be put off to the next year, the entire project may just fizzle out and I had waited too long to let this opportunity slip by. Our preparation time was further reduced by my decision to mount our expedition during the spring, i.e. prior to the onset of the monsoons. In view of the massive preparations required, some people suggested that we go in September during the post-monsoon period, but having studied the meteorological data of the region, I felt this offered little hope of success.

The selection of the climbing season is invariably among the first major decisions for the leader of any major Himalayan expedition, and often a crucial one for the ultimate success of the venture. Basically, one can either go before the monsoons or after. There is no third choice, for winters are hellishly cold and fresh snow makes climbing well-nigh impossible. And the monsoons are far too dangerous. Both the pre-monsoon and the post-monsoon seasons have almost identical balance-sheets of advantages and disadvantages to choose from. As described earlier, the weather on Kanchenjunga is far more unpredictable than on other Himalayan giants. In addition, the winter snows melt late in spring and begin very early in autumn making the climbing periods the shortest on this mountain compared with those on the other mountains in the Himalayas. This factor greatly aggravates the difficulty posed by the objective dangers and the high altitude of Kanchenjunga. In view of all this, the choice of the season for our expedition was a very difficult and crucial decision for me.

In an effort to make my gamble as scientific as possible—ultimately the choice of the climbing season is a gamble however methodically one may take the decision—I pored over vast quantities of data in an attempt to determine the pattern of the onset of monsoons in the Kanchenjunga region. I also studied the accounts of all those who had previously climbed in this area. While one assumes that autumn would be clear, the weather sometimes remains inclement even into October. In 1968 for example, it rained and snowed uninterruptedly for three days, bringing unforgettable misery to the inhabitants. Almost every bridge in Sikkim was smashed and washed away by the torrents and even the great Teesta bridge, which is 90 feet above the water level, could not stand the awful strain. The floods in the Teesta claimed 5,000 victims. I was at that time on the western slopes of the Kanchenjunga massif. The return journey was a nightmare— the roads had sunk more than 200 feet and a village was buried under the landslides. Little rivulets were overnight transformed into raging rivers carrying huge boulders.

Around the same time in 1929, the German expedition had experienced 7 feet of snow in one night and were fortunate to escape without casualties. Lord Hunt also talks of similar conditions in 1937. Freshfield and Hooker had also mentioned of unstable weather conditions during this period.

W.W. Graham, the pioneer of Sikkim expeditions, had also advocated autumn and had written, "May was the avalanche month. Furthermore, it should be noted that all the big climbs in Sikkim have been done during or after the monsoon."

Should I follow Graham's advice as the German expedition had? Or should I, knowing the erratic weather of this area's post-monsoon season, follow my own inclinations? If the summit attempt was to be made in October, the lower parts of the mountain had to be covered in September when the monsoons would still be active. If the attempt were delayed by fate or chance, we could run into winter and the awful westerlies on the North Ridge. Even the days would be shorter, climbing time limited, and the temperature very low. Yet, added to Graham's advice was another factor in favour of the post-monsoon season. Paul Bauer, the leader of the German Kanchenjunga expedition, had selected the post-monsoon season even in 1931 for the second attempt despite the fact that they had been mauled by the weather in 1929.

The pre-monsoon season has two major disadvantages which must be taken into account. First, as mentioned earlier, there is the difficulty of setting up the base camp soon enough; and second, there is the race with the monsoons. In 1955, the British expedition had sailed in the early spring, and even so had a neck-to-neck race with the monsoons.

Another phenomenon, which has not been mentioned earlier but became a special plague for us was that of frequent white-out conditions. Almost every day after nine in the morning, the mountain would be enshrouded in fog and cloud, reducing visibility to a negligible distance. A man on the rope could not see another one only 30 feet away. Route-finding in such adverse conditions becomes nearly impossible. Even movement on a trodden route is difficult due to the wind-obliterated tracks. Perhaps this is peculiar only to the eastern route which lies near Sikkim and the foothills. Such conditions are perhaps found only during the pre-monsoon season, as the German expedition which went after the monsoons, made no mention of it.

Nevertheless, after brooding for a long time I decided to put up with the inconvenience of an early start and prepared to go in spring. An added advantage of this course was that if we failed, we could always go back in autumn. Having made this first major decision, we immediately began preparations.

The Kanchenjunga Cell at the Army Headquarters now became the nerve-centre of frenzied activity to meet deadlines. Essential work such as collection of equipment, selection of sherpas, food, signal equipment and oxygen, transportation of the entire equipment to the road-head, etc, had to be coordinated and completed on time. Our selected team consisted of 16 climbing members, two doctors, a cameraman from the Films Division of India, a press reporter, two signalmen, one nursing assistant and a high-altitude support party of 37. And then there was the other major task of providing clothing, food and tentage for four months for these 60 people on the mountain.

Few people realize that a major Himalayan expedition costs millions of rupees to organize. The American expedition to Kanchenjunga-2 had cost over three million rupees and the 1975 British Everest expedition had had a budget of nearly two million rupees. Although the Army was providing most of our requirements, like food, basic equipment, transport, etc, we still needed at the very least half a million rupees to buy some essential equipment as well as to meet the other cash expenses. We proceeded to raise this money through a series of ingenious means. First we requested the Southern Command of the Army to organize a film premiere which fetched us a hundred thousand rupees. The Eastern Command organized a horse tattoo and gave us an outright grant of another hundred thousand rupees. Through a brochure we issued in Delhi, we managed to raise a further hundred thousand. This still left a deficit of two hundred thousand rupees which we planned to meet by writing articles and books, once the expedition was over.

Despite all these efforts, our budget would hardly have been sufficient for the large expedition we had planned and we had to innovate a great deal. Mountaineering equipment is so expensive that to adequately kit just 60 climbers for high altitudes would have cost us four hundred thousand rupees without considering other heavy equipment, like tents, ropes, etc. We could ill afford this. Therefore I decided we would use indigenous high-altitude Army equipment upto the height of 20,000 feet, and cut down the use of sophisticated imported equipment to the bare minimum.

Having decided this, we then concentrated on borrowing imported equipment from various sources. H.C. Sarin helped us out and loaned us some equipment from the Indian Mountaineering Foundation. The sherpas of Nepal proved another excellent bet for our shoe-string shopping budget. All foreign expeditions are required by law to provide a complete set of personal clothing to the sherpas employed by them. Most of the expeditions also leave behind a lot of equipment with these sherpas as it is quite expensive to air-freight it back. Sherpas sell such stuff at half prices in Nepal and we purchased a part of our requirement from this source. But we still needed to import a lot of equipment which would have been well-nigh impossible, had the Government of India not come to our rescue. The bureaucratic wheels turned really fast and we got our import licences and foreign exchange within a week. The Chief Controller of Exports & Imports was very helpful in exempting us from import duty on our equipment. Air India pitched in and air-lifted our equipment from all parts of the world free of cost.

These efforts resulted in our collecting all the equipment we needed. But due to our budgetary considerations, we ended up carrying two sets of equipment; one set for the low altitudes and the other for altitudes above 20,000 feet. As was to be expected, such an arrangement did not work very satisfactorily. Every time a climber or a sherpa came down from the higher camps to Camp I, he had to strip and hand over his high-altitude equipment to climbers going up. This caused a lot of resentment, especially among the sherpas, who are used to big foreign expeditions that not only provided a complete set of equipment to everyone, but also gifted this to the sherpas after the expedition. Also, since this high-altitude equipment was not the specific charge of any one climber, it was not properly looked after. However, this was the best we could manage under the circumstances.

The next major headache was oxygen. No one had yet succeeded in climbing a mountain of 28,000 feet or more without oxygen, and we were not planning to be an exception. I had worked out our requirement as approximately 150 bottles, each costing Rs. 1,500. We could hardly afford this expense. I made frantic enquiries to find out if any empty bottles were available in India. Major S. Sen, our Medical Officer, who had been collecting medicines from the Army Medical Stores mentioned to me one day that he had seen hundreds of oxygen bottles of various sizes lying at the Army Medical Stores. At first I thought these must be the heavier ones which would do no good for us. But I was in a desperate situation and decided to have a look at them anyway. We rushed to the stores about 12 miles away and found a large heap of empty oxygen bottles of various sizes, and in one small corner about 150 oxygen bottles of the type we were looking for. These had been made in France and were similar to the ones we had used on Everest. We sent Surjit to Calcutta to have them refilled from the Indian Oxygen Limited. But I was still worried about how these would perform. Group-Captain A.J.S. Grewal, Principal of the Himalayan Mountaineering Institute at Darjeeling had told me that he had tried refilled bottles but their pressure invariably dropped within a couple of months. This was a serious problem and could have disastrous effects on our final assault plans.

I worried over this till I thought of trying with the sherpas of Nepal, who might obviously have some original unused bottles. So I immediately contacted Colonel J.O.M. Roberts, a well-known mountaineer in Nepal, and he arranged for 50 such bottles that had been left behind by the 1975 British Everest expedition. This was indeed a real stroke of luck, for apart from the financial problems in importing oxygen bottles, it would have been impossible for us to get them in time by sea, as international law prohibits air-freighting of filled oxygen bottles. A further last moment snag cropped up when we found our French regulators would not fit the British bottles. The problem was however easily solved by the Electrical and Mechanical Engineers of the Army who made new adaptors for us.

Our next problem was finding the right type of food. In the West this would have been no problem as different type of food is available in tins and in dehydrated state, even pre-cooked. But the food we normally eat in India is heavy to carry and takes a long time to cook at high altitudes where atmospheric pressure is low. Also, most of our diet items are such as cannot be dehydrated. The Defence Food Laboratories experiment in dehydration of uncooked food. They helped us a little by dehydrating some food for us. But the quantities they could supply were so limited that these were sufficient only for the very high camps. Yet whatever they gave us was good and proved very useful.

To facilitate the handling of our food, Kiran, our food member, packed it into 4-man-day compo rations in specially manufactured card-board boxes. By doing this, we believed we had found a foolproof solution to the packing problem. However, when these compo-boxes were opened at higher camps we found them badly depleted. The porters had removed the straps from around the packs and pilfered items like cheese, tinned fruits, etc; we had to re-sort and repack the whole thing again at Camp I.

Our photography requirements also gave us a lot of headaches. The cameras were extremely expensive and films, not easily available. With great difficulty I was able to arrange one Asahi Pentax, complete with all attachments and accessories. The only other good camera we had was my personal Nikormat. We also carried two small electronic Yashikas. Then we ran into a problem with films. We had requested someone in London to send us colour films, but through some misunderstanding, instead of Kodachrome, he sent Kodacolour which is quite good for prints but we wanted slides. After quite an effort, I was able to buy 20

Ektachrome films which somewhat saved the situation. Thus, in all we had 20 Ektachromes, 50 Kodacolour and 20 black and white rolls. Compared with any other expedition this was chicken-feed. But as it turned out our photo coverage was not bad at all.

The problem of selecting good sherpas still remained. I made a dash to Kathmandu to seek the help of Colonel J.O.M. Roberts, who had helped us hire some sherpas for our 1965 Everest expedition that had succeeded in putting nine members on the summit, and had made a big impact in Nepal. This time too, Colonel Roberts spared no effort in helping us out. He flew from Pokhra, where he lives, to Kathmandu to meet me. He gave me 15 sherpas but I needed 40. Greatly disappointed, I then tried Darjeeling. Once the home of sherpas, Darjeeling has now very few of them. Most of the good ones have taken up permanent jobs with organizations operating in the mountains and I could muster only six more sherpas from there. Looking for high-altitude porters in other possible corners, I sent Prem to Lahul and Spiti Valley in Himachal Pradesh, and he found five more men but we were still at least 14 sherpas short and I was at a dead end.

Suddenly it struck me that the people of Ladakh live at almost the same altitude as the sherpas of Solu Khumbu. Ladakhis should therefore have similar lung adaptability as the sherpas. With nothing to lose, I decided to try 10 persons from the Ladakh Scouts, a unit of the Army, as support party to ferry loads to higher camps. As it turned out, this experiment proved successful.

There is also normally a great shortage of porters for the approach work all over the Himalayas, except in Nepal. The Indo-French Nanda Devi Traverse expedition of 1967 had been compelled to use helicopters for ferrying their stores from Joshimath to the Nanda Devi Sanctuary on account of this problem. The shortage is perhaps most severe in North Sikkim. We hired porters from Lachen, Gangtok and Darjeeling—but just to be on the safe side we also arranged with the Indian Air Force to stand by to give us air-support if needed. This precaution later proved a saviour in a grim situation. We tied up with Meteorological Department and All India Radio, Delhi, for daily weather forecasts.

All our preparations were now nearly complete. We had only to move our luggage from Delhi to Siliguri, then arrange its transport to Lachen. This was fairly easy. In all, the preparations had taken us a bare, though very hectic, three months. It would not have been possible without the generous help of our friends in India and abroad, and the stout and dependable backing of the Indian Army.

Porters being hired at Lachen.

6

The Closed Valley

Move to the Base Camp

As the preparations dragged on with no end in sight, I started getting restless and anxious. Finally, in desperation I decided that we would leave Delhi on March 7, 1977, regardless of the state of our preparations. Any start later than that would cut into the time available for our attempt before the monsoons. Once this date was decided, everything started moving faster. On March 1, an advance party under Major Pushkar Chand was despatched to open our route to the Base Camp, and also to dump rations for the porters at various stages of the approach march. The main party left Delhi a week later. I had decided to stay back for another week to supervise manufacture of the special adapters for the British oxygen bottles and attend to some other last minute tasks.

When I went to the railway station to see off the main party, I was surprised to find that three officers, some JCOs and men of the 3rd Kumaon (Rifles) had come to give the team a grand ceremonial send-off, complete with their pipers playing the farewell tune. They had also brought flowers and garlands for every member of the team, more so for me, since I belonged to their battalion. The whole ceremony was quite touching, and also rather embarrassing for me as I was not actually leaving that night. They did not know this and to tell them then would

FACING: *Ferrying loads through the Ice Fall.*

56

have been a poor anti-climax to their grand gesture. So I got on the train with the others and quietly slipped off from the other side as the train started moving!

Meanwhile, despite best efforts, Pushkar's party had only got to the second stage, Poke, after 8 days. The heavy spring snows had made the going very tough and tedious. They had come back to Lachen on March 7 for reinforcements, when the main party also reached there on March 12 and found that the snowline started from the Zemu bridge itself. There was about 3 to 4 feet of snow throughout, and it would become soggy as the day advanced. The heavily laden porters sank knee-deep at every step. The dense virgin forest, which had been a pleasure to journey through in early winter, was now a hard trial for every one. My decision to come to the mountain in the pre-monsoon period now came in for a great deal of comment from the members who started referring to it as 'Kumar's Folly'.

Our greatest tormentors were the creepers that covered the fallen trees. Like human beings, trees also suffer from over-crowding. Consequently in a dense forest, only the tallest of the trees can catch sunshine and survive. The others, which lose this struggle for the life-giving sun, die under the shadow of the taller trees. Withered, they stand for a while like ghosts among the surviving giants. Then inevitably they fall and are soon covered by parasite creepers. Now lying concealed under snow, these fallen tree trunks were discovered only when someone got his leg entangled in them. Further, since the track was covered by snow, our sense of direction was vague. Many a time, the party would take a wrong turn and get stuck in thickets of rhododendrons and then retreat and grope for the track again. The landslides which had been bad enough in autumn, now became a real hazard, particularly as the sun grew stronger and the frozen snow thawed. It was little wonder then that on the first attempt the porters refused to go beyond Poke.

I left Delhi on March 15. My wife Mridula and sister Saroj had come to see me off. It was the first time I had seen Mridula a little worried. I do not blame her for she had of course heard many knowledgeable quarters openly criticizing me for having undertaken a reckless venture.

At Siliguri, Major Bhupinder Singh, our Liaison Officer, gave me the bad news that one of our trucks had fallen into a ditch. The driver was badly hurt and though Havildar Sukhvinder Singh, one of the members who had been travelling in the truck, had got off with minor injuries, he was in hospital. Doubtful of his ability to rejoin the expedition, I called up our reserve, Havildar Khushal Singh, to accompany us to Lachen. Another piece of bad news awaited me at Gangtok. Major S. Sen, our senior doctor and considerably experienced moun-

FACING: (Above) *Near the top of the Ice Fall.* (Below) *The Ice Fall covered all approaches to the upper basin of the Zemu Glacier.*

59

taineer, was down with chicken-pox and hospitalized. This could indeed be a big blow to our chances.

I was still brooding over this when Capt Bahuguna's sister Mrs Kala, who was staying in Gangtok, came to see me. She had already lost one brother Harsha Bahuguna on Everest, and was quite upset by the local belief that the present expedition had aroused the wrath of Kanchenjunga and was bound to meet with a terrible end. The moment she entered my room, she burst into tears and pleaded for the life of her second brother. I myself had had great hesitation in including Jai in the team in the first place, precisely for this reason. Seeing her in tears my own cousin, Mrs Toshi Sudan, also started crying and I was hard put to pacify them. My entry into Sikkim seemed ill-fated and I left for Lachen with a heavy heart. Misfortune dogged me to Lachen too. Within two days, I was taken seriously ill with some strange virus infection and was in coma for a couple of days.

Meanwhile, the expedition also seemed stuck along the route to the Base Camp. Frantic at the delay, I asked Pushkar to go ahead to the Base Camp with a small party and start work on the route. In his absence, young Jai took charge of the porters. There were about 1,000 loads in all but not all were required to be moved immediately to the Base Camp. Jai had arranged the loads in neat lines and prepared proper lists, but when he asked the porters to pick these up they did not stir. After some persuasion they agreed to carry the loads but when Jai took up his position at the gate to check each one against the muster roll, all the porters quietly slunk off to their houses. I was furious but helpless to do anything. Finding no ready solution to our predicament, we approached the Sikkim government for help. The administration of Sikkim very kindly rushed John Phurba Tsering, the Deputy Commissioner of Lachen, to the spot. He used to be a school teacher before joining the administration and proved very helpful. "John, we are paying them more," I appealed to the Deputy Commissioner, "giving them light loads to carry, and providing them with winter clothing. Why then this trouble?" He sent for an elderly porter called Chhujila who had been a head-man for 15 years before losing in the recent village elections. They conversed with each other in Bhutia for a couple of minutes and then John turned to me with a smile on his face and said, "They have nothing against wages and loads, but they don't trust your load distribution and want to distribute the loads themselves according to their own choice."

"But we are following the normal organized system," I protested in a puzzled tone.

"Maybe, but they want to follow their own system."

I had no choice but to agree and follow their 'system'. Upon hearing this all the porters at once came out of their houses and collected near the loads. They were all divided under four sirdars or chiefs. The sirdars then split the entire luggage into four stacks. Then they drew lots to decide which stack should be carried by which sirdar's party. Once this was decided each sirdar collected his men around his stack and the men in turn drew lots with the help of some marked sticks and, finally after 3 hours, the 'system' had not only decided each porter's load but also put all of them in very good humour. They all laughed and patted each other on the back with the loudest applause reserved for those who had drawn the bulkiest looking loads. Having picked up their loads, the porters then disappeared into their houses leaving me very anxious for the safety of our stuff. I felt relieved only when they finally took to the road, escorted by the members of our team.

But our relief was short lived, for by the time we reached the Zemu bridge, the porters had removed the plastic linings that covered all the boxes and hidden it under their garments. We had specially wrapped this lining to keep the cardboard boxes dry. It was difficult to check everyone in a caravan spread over half a mile and we had no option but to philosophically accept this 'system' too!

The next day 150 additional porters arrived from Darjeeling. They looked very docile and carried whatever we gave them. I was quite happy. My joy however was soon cut short when most of them were back at Lachen in two days. Obviously they had encountered snow and muttered, 'We have not come to die in snow!' All our reasoning and persuasion were of no avail. Major S.S. Singh, who belongs to the Gurkha Regiment then took over and talked to them in their language, Gorkhali. In the evening he gave them a goat to slaughter, some rum and organized them to sing and dance. Good food coupled with free drinks soon created a convivial atmosphere and lit up the morose faces of the porters. Surjit (Major Singh) quickly became the most popular figure around. They exchanged jokes with him, sang songs in his praise and danced around him to express their appreciation. We felt we had solved the problem. Alas, we were sadly mistaken.

The next day all the porters were preparing to return; the clever ones had already left. I had no option but to request a para-drop of our basic food items like flour, rice, *dal*, etc. But this solved only a part of our problem since the entire equipment, oxygen and compo-boxes had still to be ferried by porters. The following signal that I sent on the afternoon of April 5 explains our plight:

. . . . . . (.) EXPEDITION LOADS SPREAD OVER AS FOLLOWS (.) ALFA (.) LACHEN (.) ONE HUNDRED AND FIFTY (.) BRAVO (.) POKE (.) HUNDRED (.) CHARLIE (.) HALF WAY BETWEEN POKE AND REST CAMP (.) FIFTY (.) DELTA (.) REST CAMP (.) FIFTY (.) PORTERS AVAILABLE APPROXIMATELY HUNDRED (.) THREE MEMBERS SPREAD OVER VARIOUS STAGES TO LOOK AFTER LIFTING OF LOADS (.)

Before I left Lachen, Chhujila advised me to have special prayers conducted for three days in the Lachen *Gompa* (Buddhist temple). I readily agreed in order to appease the religious sentiments of the local people and also hoped that the prayers might solve our porter mess! This required that we arrange to feed 15 lamas for 3 days, and also pay Rs. 100 as our offering to them, besides spending a lot of money for *ghee* (refined butter oil) used in the prayer ceremonies. After the prayers were over, we were allowed inside the *gompa*. This *gompa* is situated at the highest point on the northern edge of the village. It has a big lawn with many tall poles streaming with tiny multi-coloured prayer flags fluttering merrily in the breeze, carrying their prayers to heaven. In the centre, the main prayer flag was hoisted on a 30-foot high pole erected on a strong round platform.

The *gompa* was a straight and simple structure with mud walls and a thatched roof. The plinth of the building was raised above the ground level. So one had to climb a few steps to get into the porch which had rows of prayer wheels. There were two long tables, each about a foot high, stretching from the doorway to the altar. On these tables sat lamas in prayer. The prayers are usually so long that lamas take their food and meals while praying. They sat facing each other, about 4 feet apart. In the intervening space were two big drums, each about 2 feet in diameter, with coloured wooden handles. These drums, called *n'ga*, were beaten by drum-sticks shaped like sickles.

The moment we entered the *gompa*, two of the lamas started beating the drums. The prayer went on and after some time the lamas sitting near the altar started clanging cymbals called *si-nyen*. Then we were taken up to the altar which was dimly lit with some butter lamps. The images of Guru Rimpoche and the Kanchenjunga deity were placed in front of the altar. I placed a silken scarf, *khada*, at the foot of the central figure of Guru Rimpoche. The Kanchenjunga image was modelled with its five peaks symbolizing the five treasures of the snow. I placed another *khada* and some money at the foot of the Kanchenjunga idol. I was quite intrigued to see a wall that had many pigeon holes full of old books, perhaps containing ancient holy texts. The Head Lama was not present and since none of the other lamas knew Hindi well, we could not learn the history of this *gompa*. I felt happy after the prayers and requested the lamas to pray to Lord Kanchenjunga not to be angry with us. After the ceremony was over, we were taken upstairs and shown a collection of hundreds of paintings of the Buddha.

The lawns of the monastery fall away steeply on the village side and a young lama blew on a *dhonkar* (a conch shell) and then threw some flowers in the air. These were the blessings of the god for the entire village. As we came out of the monastery, we were each handed a bamboo cylinder lined with silver and with straws tucked in. These cylinders were filled with a drink called *tumba*, which is made of fermented millet and tastes like beer, though it is stronger in effect. The lamas diluted the drink with hot water and when we had sipped some, would again fill the cylinders to the top. It was really heady and even Prem, who seldom drinks, liked it very much.

We were perhaps the last visitors to this *gompa* which was one of the oldest monasteries in northern Sikkim, for when I was at Camp IV, I got the news that it was being pulled down to be replaced by a new building. As a consequence, all our porters deserted us for a while and went to work for the monastery as otherwise they would have had to pay a heavy fine to the lamas.

The Base Camp

On March 17, the first party under Pushkar finally established our Base Camp in the Green Lake area, just opposite the site of the old German Base Camp. As we moved towards the Base Camp, I was surprised to note that there was much less snow in this treeless area than there was in the thick jungle which we had to cross from Lachen to the Rest Camp. During our movement through this area, there was an avalanche but luckily nobody was involved. It is perhaps the only time in the history of mountaineering that an expedition encountered an avalanche on the very first day of its approach march. Normally, one has to face these hazards after the Base Camp or Advance Base Camp.

During my march from Lachen to the Base Camp, I saw many pheasants, some of which I could recognize as Monal and Blood pheasants, and also many partridges. At one place my porter pointed out to me the pugmarks of snow-leopard. This area is full of wild life but I had strictly forbidden any shooting. Thus when at one of the stages where we camped I was served delicious pheasant meat I was intrigued. On enquiry, I got the innocent reply that it had not been shot but killed with a stone!

63

7

The Ice Fall

Base to Camp I

We had a lovely site for our Base Camp, well protected from the wind and favoured by an early sun. However, the Green Lake indicated on the map of this region did not exist, and there was only a dirty brown pond nearby which could not be called a lake by any stretch of imagination. Maybe the topography of the area has changed since the Germans visited it half a century ago, or maybe we were too early in the year and the lake formed only after the monsoons. Whatever be the reason, getting water at the Base Camp became a serious problem. We had to fetch it from more than a quarter of a mile away and as the snowline receded, we had to fetch it from half a mile and even this source was fast dwindling by the time the expedition ended.

Nevertheless, a fairly big camp with mess tents, tarpaulins, wireless aerials, stocks of loads, a small meteorological observatory and a herd of grazing bharal (blue sheep) sprang up at this site.

On March 25, Prem and Nirmal opened up the route to the Advance Base Camp and established it at the junction of the Twins Glacier and Zemu Glacier at an altitude of 16,750 feet. This was about half a mile short of the old German Camp VI, which had been set up just below the eastern ridge of the North-East Spur. The route to the Advance Base Camp was a difficult one and lay over the Zemu Glacier. The moraine of a glacier can be very deceptive, a small bulge may well turn out to be a treacherous mound with a formidable scree slope behind it. There was also a lot of debris and ice waste all over. Skirting through a maze of boulders and mounds, many members lost their way at one time or another. The Germans had taken 3 days to find a route through the glacier, but once the route was made and marked even Bhutia girls, with their *bakus* (skirts) tucked up, merrily went up and down in 5 hours' time.

The Zemu Glacier is fittingly the biggest glacier in the Eastern Himalayas. Nearly 10 miles long, two-thirds of a mile wide and more than a 100 yards wide at an average, it is also the fastest receding glacier of the region. A maze of smaller rivers of frozen ice merge into the Zemu from all sides. Three glaciers with their own ice falls flow down from Simvo. The Twins Glacier, with a very broken ice mass is much whiter than the Zemu which is spotted by dirty moraine, has four tributary glaciers falling into it from the Sugar Loaf side. Then there is the Tent Peak Glacier, the biggest tributary of Zemu. Above the Base Camp, we could see another giant glacier. It must have joined into the Zemu a long time ago but now it has receded and retired to higher slopes.

Advance Base was quite an uncomfortable place due to the large number of sharp stones that made sleeping an ordeal. Apart from these difficulties, it was interesting going through this phantom land. There were huge ice caves as big as *gompas* and many beautiful glacial lakes. Huge boulders weighing hundreds of tons were precariously balanced on thin ice stems. Unlike at the Base Camp, here we had plenty of clean water from the numerous glacier ponds.

This camp was situated opposite the famous Zemu Gap which lies between the Simvo Peak and the South Summit of Kanchenjunga. First visited from this side by Dr Kellas in 1910, the 1929 German expedition had thought of climbing Kanchenjunga from the Zemu Gap after failing to make much headway on the North-East Spur. Dangerous snow conditions had turned them back. I had always been deeply interested in the ridge leading upto Zemu Gap and then on to the 27,808-foot (8,476 metres) high South Summit of Kanchenjunga, the highest unclimbed mountain in the world at the moment.

From the Advance Base Camp, the Zemu Glacier heads straight towards the Zemu Gap for about half a mile and then takes a complete ninety degree turn to the right. From around this bend we had our first uninterrupted and awe-inspiring view of the Kanchenjunga massif—an amphitheatre of rock and ice, rising 7,000 feet in sheer precipices; each precipice festooned with hanging glaciers, occasionally discharging avalanches and frozen cataracts carrying tons of debris, crashing down thousands of feet, sweeping and polishing the crags and choking the chasms on the way down.

I vividly remember the day I was taking some movie shots of members climbing in this area, when I was startled by a loud crack and turned to find that a whole mass of ice had started breaking off the East Ridge. Slowly it tore from the mountain and came tumbling down, gathering speed until it smashed on the ground with a noise like the blast of a small nuclear bomb. I tried to focus my camera on this fantastic scene but it was all over before I could move. Disappointed, I was about to put the camera away when yet another avalanche started from Simvo, with a roar like that of a thousand tigers. It seemed as if a whole side of the mountain had come off. The avalanche kept pouring down for a long time and I kept on taking the fantastic scene on the film.

Starting from the slopes of the main summit of Kanchenjunga, the South Summit and the East Summit, the Zemu Glacier traces a network of crevasses on its way down, and the sides of the glacier are dotted with huge cones of avalanche debris. It then topples over a steep rock face for some 700 feet and into a labyrinth of ice, forming a monstrous ice fall as it squeezes through the gap between the East Ridge and the North-East Spur. Imagine to yourself the Niagra Falls in a frozen state and you have a picture of the Zemu Ice Fall. There is a large rock formation in the middle of the Ice Fall, which the Germans had called 'Rock Island'. Only the eastern face of the Rock Island is visible, which is a straight wall of 500 feet with a little overhang at the top. The Rock Island divides the Ice Fall into two halves. The southern half is a rotten mass of ice constantly threatened not only by crumbling ice towers and opening crevasses, but also by avalanches from the face of the Eastern Ridge, and provides no route. Though the northern half had some cracks in its defences, it was far from safe.

On March 26, Capt Cruz tried one of these openings and went up nearly half way to the top of the Ice Fall but while returning, he was surprised to find no traces of the rope he had fixed on his way up. So we gave up this route which had been roughly in the centre of the northern half. The true left side of the glacier was also out. However, after two days of struggle, the route through the Ice Fall was finally opened on March 31 by Prem and N.D. While descending, N.D. fell into a crevasse and was in deep freeze for quite some time before being rescued. They also found a piece of rope fixed by one of the German expeditions. It had apparently moved down with the glacier. It was a hemp rope, one-and-a-half inch thick. The day they opened this route, Prem reported, "Very unstable Ice Fall. The most dangerous in the Himalayas." I have been through the Khumbu Ice Fall on Everest dozens of times and fully agree with Prem that the Zemu Ice Fall is among the most dangerous falls in the Himalayas; though neither technically very difficult, nor very long.

To negotiate the Ice Fall, our route ran for about 300 yards parallel to an ice mass on the north of the Glacier. This ice mass frequently kept discharging boulders and the area was littered with fallen ice masses. After that the route climbed up to the foot of the Rock Island and for about 100 yards it was directly under an extremely unstable mass of ice which was so frightening that I never looked up at it whenever I passed under it. Our sherpas always crossed this area

FACING: *An ice cave near Camp I.*

66

at a run to make certain they spent the least possible time in this 'Death Zone'.

The first time I reached the Death Zone, a huge boulder the size of Delhi's India Gate, had come off hardly half an hour before, and the track was completely covered by vast ice debris. I thanked God, and Chunje our cook for giving us tea late that morning! The rock spur leading to the foot of the Rock Island was safe from avalanches. At the foot of the granite Rock Island was our Crampon Point, the spot where we would put our crampons for the ice climb ahead. Kiran, Kura Ram, my sherpa Lakpa and two Ladakhi boys, who were accompanying us, had just taken off their rucksacks to put on their crampons, when a volley of stones came hurtling down like bullets. Every one ran helter-skelter for safety. "Stop!" I shouted, "watch the stones; duck and rush!" The first burst of stones scored only a minor hit. One of the Ladakhi boys caught a stone on his knee but escaped injury. The stone bombardment kept on for another five minutes. I could hear prayers being muttered, *"Om mani padme hum!"* We all stood still, following the course of the projectiles and ducking only when necessary. We then put on our crampons, although it was not too difficult to climb even without them once a rope had been fixed. We had to fix a ladder at a small ice-wall and there were two or three steep pitches, but no major problem. Beyond the Ice Fall, the glacier was level and dotted with many small frozen lakes. Our Camp I lay about 500 yards beyond the top of the Ice Fall at an altitude of 18,750 feet (5,720 metres).

It started with a two-man tent but at the peak of our activity, it had grown to three big mess tents and six small tents capable of accommodating 50 people. Pushkar, Nirmal and Gurcharan Singh, who had established this camp, had made an igloo for the kitchen. As the number of people at Camp I kept increasing, so did the size of the igloo. By the time we finally abandoned the camp, this igloo was 10 feet long and 8 feet deep. Our water point was a high mound near the camp. The snow would be dug up, filled in a bag and dragged down to the kitchen to be converted into water on the stoves. Once there were 30 of us, including climbers and sherpas, there at this Camp, and the small stoves were not adequate for cooking. We tried out the Army manufactured 45-men cooker. But it generated so much heat that the floor of the kitchen started sinking. So we had to go back to the stoves. Later on we found a glacial lake nearby which served us well for water till the end. The site was normally sheltered from the wind and received sunlight as early as 6 a.m. from its open eastern approach. All in all, it was an ideal camping place.

From this camp we could also watch the progress on the Spur right up to Camp VI. We set up our signal centre for the higher camps here. Very often Camp III could not talk to Camp IV and so the messages were relayed through here.

FACING: *Major Prem Chand jumaring up to Camp II.*

An avalanche peeling off the Eastern Ridge of Kanchenjunga.

The camp was manned by Capt Cruz and he did an excellent job. He was fond of talking and hence was an ideal man for the wireless. Secondly, he was also fond of good eating and ensured that the best food on the mountain was available at this camp. He came up to this camp with the first party, and left it after two months with the last. Considering that he had not lived at high altitudes before, and that this was his first expedition, he did extremely well. Inside his tent, he set up a Medical Inspection Room, neatly laid out his medicines on the chest, and called it a one-bed hospital; the bed being the one he slept on! One night a blizzard hit this camp and many tents, including his, collapsed. He was very upset that Kanchenjunga had bombarded even his hospital!

He had another interesting hobby. When in charge of the wireless, he would continuously keep chasing our incoming mail as soon as it got to Lachen, with the result that our letters got to us in record time.

8

Which Way Up

Camp II

From Camp I, the upper basin of the Zemu Glacier ran almost level to the south face of the North-East Spur. There are a few crevasses in this 500-yard area but none very dangerous. Many of us stumbled into these at one time or another but escaped without injury.

The south face of the North-East Spur rises up almost vertically for about 800 feet from the flat glacier basin. The Germans had described it as follows:

"One thing we saw immediately, and that was that this wall was quite different from anything we had previously experienced in the Alps or in the Caucasus. The steep flank to the lowest point of the ridge was scored with innumerable ice gullies, and between them rose sharp and jagged ridges crowned with cornices. A traverse of the broken face that looked possible to us yesterday was now clearly seen to be out of question. We tried to climb straight up but before long the whole party was stung out one above another on the slabs but without any possibility of belaying and quite unable to go on ... The wall was becoming exceptionally difficult and it was obviously impossible for us all to get up. In addition last five men were in acute peril from the falling stones. Then the five men came down and two of them proceeded without packs."

And then:

"Even climbing light they did not succeed and finally vertical slabs and deceptive cornices made it impossible for them to go on."

71

Pushkar and party made many reconnaissance trips up and down the glacier before they selected a straight line up the gully where Schaller and Pasang Sherpa had fallen off and died. At the bottom of this gully, there is a very huge avalanche cone. Gurcharan negotiated the vertical rock next to the cone and then traversed to the top of the cone. Later when I went to this place I found that the area below the cone was a deadly crevasse field. One had only to peep through any small hole in the artificial snow bridge to see deep ice caves. There were chasms as far as the eye could see. From the top of the cone, Pushkar's party passed over glazed rocks and then kept to the rocks on the right of the gully. It was a daring probe. They had gone without crampons and had perforce to keep to the rocks.

Down at the Base Camp, I was very anxiously awaiting the outcome of this first step towards the Spur. This would tell us if we were on the right track. The party made excellent progress till they got near the crest. They could not climb the final ice pitch without crampons and so they returned. But they had mastered the face and the only 50 odd yards remained to a little ice shelf which was to serve as our Camp II.

Prem and Kiran went up to establish this camp next day and made the route up this last bit. There was great jubilation at the Base Camp when they gained the ridge. Dr Cruz ordered *halva* (an Indian sweet dish) and cheese *pakoras* (fried cheese with grain flour). Someone even suggested a sip of our medicinal brandy. The sherpas and Ladakhi boys found this a good excuse to pinch the Lachen girls in celebration of the occasion. I knew the difficult task was yet to begin but at least we had got a toe-hold on the North-East Spur. That evening I told Arun Dhar,

The North-East Spur with an arrow showing Camp III. The Twins Glacier is in the background.

the Samachar reporter, that it was too early to say anything but the next four or five days would tell us whether we would make it or not. It would either be all over soon or it would be a very long drawn out struggle.

Kiran's party consisting of Norbu, Kura Ram and Sukhvinder Singh besides himself was selected for the honour of 'cutting the first ice' on the ridge. In 1929, Allwein and Thoenes had got to this point, taken one look at the ridge and returned to say, "... definitely that the ridge itself, which was crowned with snow cornices from 30 to 60 feet high and which overhung on the far side about 300 feet and then fell away vertically for over 3,000 feet was impracticable". Paul Bauer was very depressed and ordered a reconnaissance to find out the possibility of an alternate route from the Zemu gap.

On April 7, Kiran's party moved into the camp on the ridge. I sent the following message to the Army Headquarters:

KANCHENJUNGA SITREP (SITUATION REPORT) (.) CAMP II OCCUPIED BY KUMAR'S PARTY WITH VIEW TO MAKE ROUTE THROUGH THE ICE RIDGE (.) THIS IS MOST CRUCIAL STAGE OF THE EXPEDITION (.) WEATHER REMAINED BAD (.)

The next day, I moved up to the Advance Base Camp and received Prem's message from Camp I: "I have found a shorter route to the ridge. It would also avoid the horizontal traverse." I asked him to continue his reconnaissance. Prem was trying a route the Germans had stated to be impossible, describing it as "traversing along the face with all its gullies shooting avalanches and falling

The route on the South face of the North-East Spur. Camp I is seen in the foreground.

stones." On the other hand Kiran reported after the day's work on the ridge, "We are working hard at those ice towers but fresh snow is playing havoc." On this score however, I was more worried about Prem who was working at a lower altitude than Kiran who was out of avalanche zone.

On April 9, I went up to Camp I. The day was clear and before entering the camp, I chanced to look towards the horizontal traverse and stopped dead with fright: two dots were precariously perched on the pinnacle, clinging to the ice like spiders. I watched them creeping up for a long time. The two men seemed stuck half way up on the fantastic climb. A little to the right I could see the Twins Glacier side of the ridge. My feet started getting cold after a while and I reluctantly moved into the camp. Prem was still away but I could not see him among the rocks.

The next day I went up to Camp II with Wangyal, a high altitude porter from Lahul-Spiti carrying a rope as a token of our ferry. Prem had very thoughtfully changed the lower bit of the route. Instead of going straight up the gully, we now went right and then traversed the gully which Allwein had followed to Eagle's Nest, the site of the German Camp VII. We halted for a long time at this historic spot. It was really a narrow and long platform sheltered by a rock which climbed into the sky. A day earlier, N.D. Sherpa had found three rusted crampons here presumably belonging to the 1931 German expedition. Now I found two frames for snow shoes and wondered what possible use the Germans had put these to on such a steep slope. There was also an old magazine which I thought I would collect on my way down, little knowing that on my way down we would be carrying the dead body of a comrade.

From the Eagle's Nest we rounded a rib and came to the gully where we saw Pushkar's route. After climbing in the gully for about 300 feet we turned to the rock face on our right. This rock face had many awkward pitches but they were all roped. I looked back and found Wangyal not using the rope at all. Twice I asked him to do so but he felt quite safe without it though it worried me, for a little slip here would lead to a fatal fall. At the foot of the steep rock face we were greeted by a small stone shower. I thought bigger rocks would follow but upon looking up I was pleasantly surprised to see Sukhvinder Singh thoughtfully coming down with some juice to receive us. I was very thirsty and drank it hanging on to the fixed rope at the spot which was later to become the site of a grievous tragedy.

After a short rest we climbed up to Camp II to find it deserted. Kiran, Kura Ram and Norbu were working on the mountain. Sukhvinder Singh brewed some tea for us and the three climbers who were on the third pinnacle, furiously taking turns at hacking away ice and snow. After some time, Kiran led the rope back to the camp, looking fatigued, their hands bleeding from cuts made by the ice and their lips parched with thirst. Long into that evening, we all sat chatting with excitement and expectation in that vast, unknown wilderness. It was Norbu's turn to cook that night and he made 'Thukpa', a Tibetan stew. I could eat only a

74

little but Kiran had a hearty meal. I was happy at this sure sign of acclimatisation. At night Kiran and I had another session discussing our prospects. "There is no place to stand there and chop off the ice," he said.

"But unless you are able to, I don't think sherpas with loads would be able to get across." I replied.

"We are trying our best to axe away as much ice as we can but let me warn you that you may still have to crawl at many places."

Next morning they started off late as they were all feeling tired. They had now been continuously labouring for 4 days at 19,000 feet. I accompanied them to their high point of the previous day. I was very impressed at the hard work they had already put in. They had cut lanes in the projecting ice masses and fixed rope bridges from one ice tower to another. The team seemed in great form. They again started hacking at the icebergs. Kiran and Norbu were supported by Kura Ram and Sukhvinder Singh. I concentrated on taking pictures. At 3 p.m. I was greatly amazed to see figures descending the steep portion of the ridge ahead of us. Prem and N.D. had made a break-through! Kiran, who was leading and was at the end of the horizontal traverse, could see and speak to them. He acted as an intermediary between Prem and I. "How was the route?" I asked.

"The leader is asking how the route was," Kiran relayed my question to Prem.

"Good," replied Prem who is a man of few words.

"Is it safe for loaded sherpas?"

"Yes."

"How does it compare with Kiran's route?" I asked

"It is better."

"Is there any danger from stones or avalanche?"

"Yes, there is. I want to go down," volunteered Prem for once. He had been working under great stress. I very much wanted to let him go as Pushkar's team was already on way to take his place. But I also wanted further information about the route from him. So I asked him to stay another night at Camp I and told him that I would meet him there the next morning. This was to prove a blessing in disguise. I then asked Kiran to stop the work on his route. "Are we following that route?" he asked me. "Most probably," I replied, "but you never know; Prem could be wrong." I asked him to leave the extra ropes there in case we had to follow this route again otherwise we could retrieve them later. Kiran and his party was disappointed as to them it was like abandoning their baby. It was getting chilly so we started back. "Can I stay a day more?" Kiran requested.

"What for?" I enquired.

"Only 20 yards of this route remain and I would like to complete at least that stretch, if only for my personal satisfaction." I told him that the mountain was very big and the climb had just started. There would be plenty of climbing for everybody. Unhappy, he agreed to pull down his team the next day.

9

Kanchenjunga Strikes

"The ways of the providence are unscrutable but there should be some reason why such young and promising life should be taken."

—Scott

I spent that night at Camp II. It was a comfortable night except for the thought that four days' labour and the risks taken by Kiran's party had gone waste. The first rays of the morning sun hit the camp at about 7 a.m. It was Sukhvinder's turn to prepare breakfast. Despite his best efforts to light the stove, it took him a long time. I was getting a little impatient because I wanted to start early and take pictures on the way down. Sukhvinder quietly bore up with my impatience and finally managed to brew some tea. We mixed it with porridge left over from the previous night's meals and hurriedly gulped it down.

Norbu was the first to get started. Sukhvinder followed. None of us were roped up since the entire route was already fix-roped. Norbu and Sukhvinder had hardly gone down 50 yards when they remembered the ice-axe they had anchored on top of an ice ridge 50 feet above. Norbu jokingly suggested to Sukhvinder that he ought to get it back. And there was Sukhvinder climbing up a thin ridge, sitting astraddle and clawing at the snow to get a good grip. In

---

FACING: *Eagle's Nest—a famous landmark on the North-East Spur.* OVERLEAF: (Above) *Climbing over the original route near the old Camp II.* (Below) *The last post at Kanchenjunga—a mountain funeral for Havildar Sukhvinder Singh.*

a few minutes he had retrieved the ice-axe. Then both of them started down again.

We started off 5 minutes later with Kiran leading, myself in the middle and Kura Ram bringing up the rear. We were taking it a little easy, possibly since we felt we had only an easy descent ahead. But Kiran does not believe in taking things easy and drives himself and everyone around him very hard. He would often needlessly overload himself and others and so I had to put my foot down when that morning he insisted on carrying 4 extra ropes. After about half an hour, we came to the spot where we had to round an ice tower that had sheer drops on all sides. I had just reached this spot when we heard a shout echoing in the mountains. I stopped dead, hanging on to the ice tower, and strained to hear better. My heart was filled with foreboding even before I heard Kiran yelling; "Help! Help!" and then desperately, "Kura, come down quick! Hurry up!" Kiran's call heightened my apprehensions. I looked at Kura Ram and he said, "Kiran is in trouble." Before we could think of anything, we saw a red rucksack hurtling down the gully, disappearing into the depths below. I recognised it as Kiran's and was certain Kiran was in bad trouble.

I told Kura Ram to take off his rucksack and rush down and I followed. My mind was a whirlwind of anxiety, concern and terrible apprehensions. Praying to God to give Kiran strength to hold on till Kura Ram reached him, I rushed down. By now a deathly silence had enveloped the slopes. There were no shouts, no echoes. A deep hollow was growing in the pit of my stomach as I thought that Kiran might have had a fatal accident. In the next 10 minutes I lived an eternity. As I rushed to the source of the distress calls, I somehow controlled myself and sobered up to face my immediate responsibility of attending to the situation as the leader.

Down at Camp I also, the shouts had been heard but the words were indistinguishable. Prem, Nirmal and Gurcharan were all confused and worried. They did not know whether they ought to go up. Then they saw someone fast descending to the camp. It was Norbu who had taken a long lead over us, and was not quite clear what had happened. On reaching Camp I he blurted out, "One of the Kumars seems to be in difficulty." This led everyone at Camp I to believe that I must have met with some accident, Kiran being so much younger and stronger.

Rounding the last corner before the disaster spot, I braced myself for the worst, but was taken aback when I saw Kiran standing there. "Are you okay?" I asked him, trying to control my overwhelming emotions.

"I'm alright!" he said in a barely audible tone. Then I saw some blood stains on the snow. "What's that?" I asked horrified. Kiran muttered something which

OVERLEAF: (Above) *Air-dropping of supplies.* (Below) *Prayer flags near Camp II. A steep snow gully leads upto a rib of the North-East Spur.* FACING: *Negotiating snow mushrooms and gullies below Camp II.*

I could not make out. Believing that Kiran had been hurt but was trying to hide it from me, I descended the last 10 yards to him. Then I saw a pair of legs in the snow and stopped dead. "Who's that?" I asked.

"Sukhvinder is hurt," replied Kiran heavily. I rushed down and saw Sukhvinder's body lying prone on the ground. His mouth was frothy and there was a lot of blood on his hands and I knew that he was not just hurt, but dead. His glove badly torn and tattered, gave evidence of the terrible struggle he must have put up to save himself. Later when we removed his gloves, we discovered that the joint between the first finger and the thumb had been deeply severed.

"When did he die?" I asked.

"He was dead when I reached here." Kiran replied. And then after a moment's awkward silence, he narrated the story. "When I was at the top of this pitch I found the rope taut as though someone was pulling it from below. I shouted down angrily but there was no response. Cursing whoever was trying to be funny, I lowered myself carefully and to my horror, found Sukhvinder entangled in the rope. His rucksack had slid around his neck. I threw away my rucksack and tried to lift him, but could not as he was badly caught up in the rope. I shouted for help. When Kura Ram arrived, we managed to untangle Sukhvinder's limp body and stretched it in the snow."

I was stunned. I tried feeling Sukhvinder's pulse and for a moment thought I could detect a faint beat. But it was only my imagination. It was now 11 a.m. and we all stood in a state of shock, unable to decide what to do next. I thanked my lucky stars that I had asked Prem's party to stay an extra night at Camp I. Pushkar, Nirmal and Gurcharan were due there early to relieve Prem's party and I hoped they would also arrive in time to help. But there was no movement yet from Camp I. It was impossible for us to carry him down on our own. We joined our voices and shouted together to attract the attention of those at Camp I, and after a while we saw a group start up.

They arrived in record time; Prem in the lead, followed by N.D. and others. "What happened?" Prem asked as he reached near. No one replied for no reply was needed. The ghastly tragedy was there for all to see. Prem knelt and felt the pulse; he too thought for a moment that he had detected a flicker, but Sukhvinder was dead. Kanchenjunga had taken its toll.

Recovering slowly from the impact of a comrade's death, I tried to get a grip on myself. Years of army discipline helped me to keep my emotions in check. The first thing was to get the body to the Base Camp. N.D., Nirmal, Gurcharan, Prem, the sherpas from Manali, Kura Ram, Kiran, all joined in the task. It was a dangerous pitch. One small avalanche in the gully and we would have had many more casualties. Also, since the fixed rope was being used by so many people at the same time, it could easily have snapped with disastrous results. But all of us were too numb at that moment to think of this.

I followed the others; my mind, a whirl of confusion. Only that morning I

82

had seen Chomalhari, and had sombrely recalled that seven years ago, three members of my team had slipped and lost their lives in the Tibetan snows. Prem and I had gone up to look for their bodies but to no avail. After that tragedy I had remained sad for months. And then this. Sukhvinder Singh had married only a few months ago. I just could not bear to think how his young bride and his old father would receive the news of his death. On the way down, we found Sukhvinder's sleeping bag which must have fallen out of his rucksack. It lay open in the snow, ready for use. For a moment I thought of picking it up, but on second thoughts I left it lying there, ready for use ...

We reached Camp I at about 5 p.m. Pushkar's party had also come up by then. He tried to make contact with the Base Camp. But troubles never strike singly and at the crucial moment the wireless set gave way. It took us one full hour to establish contact with the Base Camp. I passed on the following message:

FROM AKE (ARMY KANCHENJUNGA EXPEDITION) TO INDARMY, HIGH ALTITUDE WARFARE SCHOOL, SIKH REGIMENTAL CENTRE, 10 SIKHS, INFO: EASTERN COMMAND. IT IS WITH DEEP REGRET I INFORM YOU THAT HAVILDAR SUKHVINDER SINGH OF HIGH ALTITUDE WARFARE SCHOOL DIED OF A CLIMBING ACCIDENT AT APPROXIMATELY 1100 HOURS ON 12 APRIL. BY THE TIME HELP REACHED HIM HE WAS DEAD. HE WAS NEGOTIATING A FIXED ROPE BETWEEN CAMP II AND CAMP I WHEN THE ACCIDENT OCCURRED. HIS BODY HAS BEEN BROUGHT DOWN TO CAMP I TODAY. WE HOPE TO TAKE HIM TO THE BASE CAMP TOMORROW THE 13 APRIL. WE PLAN TO CREMATE THE BODY ON 13 OR 14 APRIL UNLESS WE HEAR FROM YOU OTHERWISE.

That night I slept in the tent next to the one in which Sukhvinder's dead body lay. I wanted to be alone for some time, for a number of things needed to be sorted out and some important decisions taken within the next couple of days. We had not even reached the deadly Spur and had already lost a man. Was the mountain worth losing precious human lives? I remembered what Barry Carbet had said at John Britenbach's death in the Khumbu Ice Fall during the American Everest expedition of 1963, "Stupid, god-damned gentleman's sport that kills people in their prime and happiness." Yes, mountaineering is sometimes a stupid god-damned sport; but more stupid and god-damned are the men in this sport who never give up. All through the night I had disturbing dreams: I was climbing Kanchenjunga, but my friends were pulling me down. It hurt like hell ...

Next morning with the help of the sherpas, we brought the body down through the Ice Fall. On the way we halted for a breather at a flat ice pitch just before the Crampon Point. We had just settled down when all hell seemed to break loose around us. There was a shower of stones from the rock overhang and an area of more than 20 square yards was peppered by falling stones. I thanked our stars that we had stopped where we did; even a couple of minutes' delay could have been fatal for all of us. Gurcharan, who is a little superstitious, said, "It was the doing of the spirits of Schaller and Sherpa Pasang, who lie buried on top of this island." In 1931, they had fallen off almost at the same spot where Sukhvinder had and their team members had buried them at the top of the Rock Island. I just kept quiet.

The party picked up Sukhvinder's body and the caravan started again. I watched with my heart in my mouth as they slowly crossed the danger zone to the Crampon Point, and over to the safe region. Greatly relieved, I got up and followed. A helicopter that had come to evacuate two members suffering from extreme high altitude sickness (Pulmonary Oedema) at the Base Camp hovered around us, then dipped its wings in salute to the first martyr of the expedition and went away to land at Base.

We could not make it to the Base Camp that day. Everyone was tired, demoralized and heart-borken. We spent the night at the Advance Base instead. The next morning another 20 porters came from the Base Camp to help carry the body down. The procession of about 50 people hobbled through the moraine of the Zemu Glacier and reached the gloomy Base Camp. To make matters worse, it started snowing, and continued so for the next 3 days.

According to the Sikh religious traditions, the last rites require recitations from the *Gutka*, a Sikh scripture, at the time the body is consigned to fire. We sent a message to Lachen to have a *Gutka* sent to us. Meanwhile, we all scoured around and collected a hundred logs of juniper. The snow kept on, and covered everything as we waited for the holy book to arrive. Capt Kohli and Surinder Singh brought it up all the way from Lachen in one day. Finally on April 18, we built a pyre near a lake and placed Havildar Sukhvinder Singh's body on it. Surinder chanted from the *Gutka* in Punjabi:

"Thus far we go with you our friend, and no further. You have a heavenly path ahead of you, and we have to suffer a little more."

Then I lit the pyre, slowly a white plume of smoke rose from the juniper, swirling upwards along the barren flanks of our mountain towards the summit of Kanchenjunga.

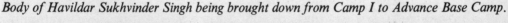

Body of Havildar Sukhvinder Singh being brought down from Camp I to Advance Base Camp.

10

Back to the Mountain
Camp III

The morale of the team had sunk very low after the tragedy. On April 16, I set up a Court of Inquiry, consisting of Major Prem Chand, Capt Dr Cruz and Capt Jai Bahuguna to determine the causes of the accident which took Havildar Sukhvinder Singh's life. After the three of them had talked to all of us who had been descending from Camp II that fateful day, they did not take long to complete their inquiry. Then I called everyone together in the mess tent. "Gentlemen, since Kiran was the first to reach the scene of the tragedy, I would like him to recapitulate what he saw." Kiran narrated what he had seen, first in English and then in Hindi for the benefit of the sherpas and porters.

"You have just heard Kiran. As per the Army regulations, I have also had an inquiry conducted and would like to inform you of the opinion formed by the Court. It is the unanimous opinion of the Court . . . that all precautions had been taken by the team to make the route safe . . . that Havildar Sukhvinder Singh was a competent mountaineer and in a fit condition to descend . . . the accident was an 'Act of God' . . . that such tragic mishaps are a part and parcel of mountaineering and that nobody is to blame for our comrade's death."

They all heard me out in silence and looked expectantly at me. I could read the question in their faces: would I call off the assault? I had not only to answer the question but also convince and carry every one of them along with me. I had struggled with this question since the day of the tragedy and had come to the decision that we had to do the job we had come for; there should be no question of retreat at the first loss. The decision had not been easy. On one hand was the thought that I had no right to risk any more lives in what was after all a sporting venture and where all the members were volunteers. We were not fighting a war, where a Commander is justified in ordering his troops to battle, realizing fully well that loss of life would be involved. On the other hand, I felt that calling off the expedition would mean Sukhvinder's supreme sacrifice had been meaningless. My mind was made up.

"Gentlemen," I addressed them, "we now have to take a crucial decision; do we carry on or not? On my part, I am clear that we must continue as I feel Sukhvinder would not have it otherwise. However, as you are all volunteers, I would like to know if any of you may want to withdraw at this stage." I first turned to Prem, who sat distractedly picking at the ground, and asked, "What do you say?" He sat motionless for a long minute, considering my question. I was anxious to know how he felt. My deputy leader on Kanchenjunga and climbing companion of many an earlier expedition, I had a great deal of faith in his judgement and knew that whatever he said could influence some of the members considerably.

He looked up finally, and said in his normal, level tones, "I see no reason to call off the expedition. Accidents like this often happen on the mountains. We are all aware of this, but climb nevertheless, I feel we must carry on." I was greatly relieved to hear Prem support my judgement. Then one by one, I turned to all the members and they were all unanimous in feeling that we had to make a serious effort to accomplish what one of us had laid his life for.

We then turned to the task ahead. Some members strongly felt that we should give up the North-East Spur route and climb the face leading directly to the North Col at the junction of the North-East Spur and the North Ridge. There was no doubt that climbing this face would have been relatively easy but the route was dangerously exposed, and just one avalanche would have been sufficient to wipe out the entire line of camps.

Others again voiced the opinion that I had selected the wrong season for the expedition. They wanted us to withdraw now and return in September. The weather was certainly appalling. We learnt later that it was an exceptional turn of weather all over the Himalayas that season. According to the reports, there had never been such heavy snowfall in the Nepal Himalayas during the last two hundred years. However, there were many in the team who wholly supported me.

Once our plan of action was affirmed, most vacillation was over and everyone started preparing for action. Some suggestions, however, did keep coming in to me to try the route up the face. For instance, Ila Tashi, our Sherpa Sirdar from Nepal, insisted that we should try this other route, since it was easier. When I explained to him the dangers we might expect on this route, he was not convinced. "Nothing else could be as dangerous as this," he said vehemently. Patiently I told him that the other route may cause a catastrophe like the one that had occurred on Nanga Parbat when 15 climbers had perished on the mountain. During another expedition to the same mountain in 1934, Ang Tshering was the only one to survive. He had personally narrated this tragic story to me in Darjeeling.

I was clear that this route was too exposed to risk. But some members persisted in suggesting that we should at least make a reconnaissance. Though my arguments had little effect, I was determined not to start reconnoitering the other route, thus dividing and distracting our efforts. No one could be expected to make a whole-hearted effort on the North-East Spur if it were known that someone was trying an easier option. So I remained firm and ruled out all such suggestions.

Obviously my decision did not please everybody. But even those who were against it took it very well and everyone put in his best. There could not be many climbers around, who would work with such dedication on a project they considered unsafe and even suicidal.

It was now the turn of Pushkar's party to go up but he was not well and Gurcharan too had a backache. On the other hand, I did not like to send Prem's party up again as it was not fair to expose them to any greater danger than the others. So I thought of going up myself but Prem would have none of it. He forced the issue and I had to let him go into the lead.

His party left for the higher camps on April 19, the day after the cremation. The rest of us carried loads to the Advance Base Camp. Prem, N.D., Dorje, Jawahar, Khushal and Dr Cruz stayed the night at the Advance Base, while we returned to the Base. On the way down we had another casualty. Surjit and I were walking on a stretch of the snow-covered moraine and I was thinking that it would be so very easy to break a leg or get a sprain if one were to slip here over a stone. The thought had barely occurred to me when I heard Surjit let out a cry. I looked back and found he had twisted his ankle and was in terrible pain. It was impossible for me to carry him all the way back and he had to limp back to Base, all the while groaning with pain.

This was another serious loss for the expedition since Surjit was a very experienced climber and a deputy leader of the team. He had scaled Kolahoi and Nun, and had skied down Trisul. I had had big hopes in him but a small stone had now ended the chances of his doing any active climbing on Kanchenjunga. However, there proved to be the proverbial silver lining to this dark cloud. After getting to

Camp II at 19,500 feet, perched on a small ledge.

Camp I, Surjit took charge of our ferries and communication with higher camps and manfully stuck to this all through the expedition. Normally, it is very difficult to find a climber who is prepared to stay back and take care of this thankless task, vital for the success of any expedition. On the 1965 Everest expedition, for instance, the doctors had restricted me from going beyond the Base Camp, on account of my frost-bitten toes. I had been then put in charge of the logistics. According to that personal experience I can say with authority that logistics play a key role in the success of any big Himalayan climb. By gaining an expert like Surjit to handle this job, albeit through a mishap, our chances certainly got a boost.

Prem now followed the new route he had selected, traversing from Eagle's Nest to the lowest depression on the North-East Spur. He put a fresh Camp II just below the Col, next to a sheer rock face. This ice overhang provided barely enough space for two small tents and no room at all for moving about. After Camp II, he followed a very steep ice gully which took him on to a southerly rib of the North-East Spur. A very thin ledge from the rib led him to the crest. At this point he was approximately 300 feet higher than the lowest point on the horizontal traverse. He then made a high-line traverse on the left, just below the crest. This area has been described as follows by James Ramsay Ulman:

"There were no rocks anywhere, no bare straightway slope of ice and snow. Instead, the North-East Spur climbed skyward for thousands of feet in one unending spine of broken, twisted ice. There were towers piled upon towers, cliff upon cliff, huge vertical columns which tapered like church spires and shining curtains, festooned with icicles, hanging down the precipices from cornices above. There was great bulges and chasms, wrenched by wind and cold into fantastic mushroom shapes and grotesque likeness of monsters from a nightmare. And as if all these were not enough the whole broken tortured expanse was swept incessantly by avalanches. Gigantic blocks and bergs of solid ice breaking off high above swept down the chutes and spirals of the spur in two-mile drops of thundering destruction."

This ridge was clearly visible from Camp I and people there could see Prem tracing a graceful route up. When I reached Camp I on April 23, Dr Cruz pointed out to me the two tiny figures crawling under the first overhanging mass of ice. My first impression was one of disbelief, which quickly changed to admiration as Dr Cruz showed me the route: the two tents of Camp II, the steep ice gully immediately to its left and from the top of the gully the route climbing over three

FACING: *The Cock's Comb Ice Ridge below Camp III.* OVERLEAF: (Above) *Camp III—an oasis on the savage, broken North-East Spur.* (Below) *Simvo massif as seen from Camp III.*

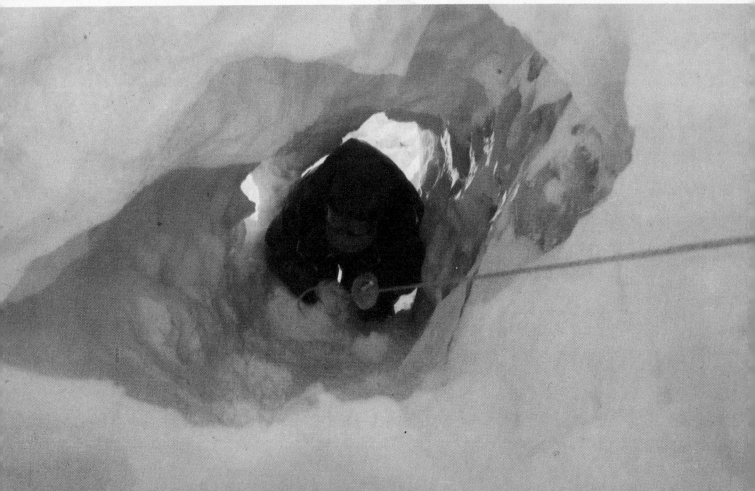

steep rocky patches, covered with snow and perched atop a 1000-foot precipice. Then there was a big ice mushroom in which I could see even from Camp I at least one deep fissure. This was slippery ground indeed and Dr Cruz told.me of a near thing on this pitch, "When one of the climbers slipped on this furrow, there was an avalanche. For a moment I thought all of them were finished. But fortunately the avalanche had passed over them." As we watched, Prem was on top of the mushroom. He stayed there for a long time, perhaps making up his mind about the route to take next.

At 3 p.m. Prem's party stopped work and returned to Camp II. An hour later, I spoke to Prem on the wireless set, "Hellow Prem, how is it going?"

"It is very risky with the soft snow. You never know when it'll slip under your feet. But with fixed rope it should be better. I had to anchor my ice-axe on the other side of the ridge." He went on to give me the discouraging news that Jawahar and Dorje had fallen ill. So the next day I replaced them with Angchuck and Khushal. But soon Khushal also fell ill and had to come down.

Down at the Base Camp, our Senior Medical Officer was having a tough time. He very much wanted to go up, but with an ever-increasing number of patients under his care he just could not stir. Three more casualties had now come down to him from Camp I: Dorje, Khushal and Jawahar. Jude had also gone down from the Advance Base and Dr Sen gave me the disturbing news that he had developed a heart condition; he was very pale and needed to be evacuated by a helicopter.

Jude was the youngest member of our team and had the reputation of being as tough as a mountain mule. He had gone through all his mountaineering courses with flying colours. I had personally seen him on Siniolchu and was greatly impressed, but now he had to be evacuated to the Siliguri hospital. I was relieved to learn later that what we thought was heart condition had only been a severe case of high-altitude sickness. Our cameraman, Naidu, too was sick at the Base Camp. He had not been feeling well for some days and kept on postponing his departure for the higher camps in the hope that some rest would set him right. But as his condition grew worse, he could not hide it any longer. The doctor sent him back too, and thus we were without a cameraman. So I took over the responsibility of shooting the movie film of the expedition. I was already the official photographer and thus not at all certain whether I could do justice to this job; but there was no alternative. Fortunately, later results disproved my fears. For the future, I am convinced that unless one can get a professional cameraman, like Norman Dyhrenfurth, who is also an excellent mountaineer, it is better to train a mountaineer as a cameraman, rather than vice-versa.

OVERLEAF: *The Monster Tower looming above Camp III.* FACING: (Above) *The Leader, Colonel Narinder Kumar.* (Below) *A tunnel on the snows of the North-East Spur.*

With Pushkar and Gurcharan added to the list, we had seven patients at the Base Camp. I remembered Eric Shipton, the pioneer of Himalayan mountaineering, had always been against large expeditions. But on a big mountain like Kanchenjunga, it is very risky to take a small party. In our case for instance, with one member dead and seven in bed, a smaller party would have been so depleted as to be forced to call off the expedition.

On April 24, Kiran, Kura Ram and Norbu started up to relieve Prem's party at Camp II. Meanwhile, Prem was at the top of the mushroom. My heart missed a beat when he appeared coming down. Had he come across some unsurmountable difficulty? From where I was watching him through my binoculars, it seemed as though he was returning. But after a few minutes I realized that he was actually attempting a horizontal traverse. Hacking away at masses of ice and wading through waist-deep snow, he made slow but sure progress. To gain every foot entailed an arduous struggle with the mountain as it resisted with chasms, avalanches, bad weather, ice blocks and sheer steepness. The climbers fought it all with courage and tenacity. I dare say that ultimately on a high mountain, these two factors outweigh all others like experience, technical expertise, equipment, physical fitness, etc. All these are undoubtedly quite essential but the first two factors are the crucial ones for victory against the heavy odds.

The experienced sherpas accompanying Prem later told me that what they saw that day was perhaps the highest standard of mountaineering they had ever seen. But as usual, Prem made no mention of his superlative effort, neglecting even to mention a near thing that Ila Tashi, the Sherpa Sirdar, later told me about, "I was belaying Major Prem Chand when he slipped starting a snow-slide. I could not have held him and had he not managed to stop himself, we would all have gone." But no word from Prem. For him it was all a part of the game!

On April 25, Kiran's party started later from Camp II and reached Prem's high point around 11 a.m. When they got to the last snow pitch, a treacherous looking one, they found the rope anchored only to an ice-axe stuck in soft snow. Kiran later complained to Prem, "I wish you had told me that the rope was tied only to your axe. I would not have risked putting my whole weight on it." Prem's reply was typically curt, "At least you had a track to follow, we had none."

Kiran did a very wise and practical thing. Finding that operating from Camp II was taking a lot of time, he established a higher camp under a big overhanging iceberg. We called it the temporary Camp III. It was the only place where at least half a tent could be pitched. From temporary Camp III, the progress was a little faster. Immediately above temporary Camp III, there was a steep ice wall which they tension-climbed and hit a thin snow ridge, one foot wide and falling sheer down to the Zemu Glacier on the left and the Twins Glacier on the right. They sat astraddle on its spine and crossed over by slowly sliding forward. Though they were belaying each climber as he crossed this ridge, yet if any one had slipped, it would have been absolutely impossible to save him. Even after this section had

94

been fix-roped, we used to take a deep breath before crossing it. As more and more climbers went across, they cut steps and kept hacking away at the ice towers to make place for their bodies and rucksacks. It was like building a road in a rock cliff. We toppled over as many mushrooms as we could to make it safe.

Kiran had a good team in the cautious Kura Ram and the dashing Norbu. Kura Ram made an excellent belay man, even though he took his turn leading. This team was excellently supported by Nima, a sherpa from Nepal, who was quite uncomplaining and dedicated. They would start their work early in the morning. Nima would prepare breakfast for them and carry it to the scene of operations. Work on ice consumes a lot of time and strength. The worst part of it is that the man who is not working has to stand, getting colder and banging his feet on ice to keep them warm and safe from frost-bite. It would usually start snowing after about 10 a.m. and then they had to contend with flying snow flakes that would get into their eyes and ears. The one favourable factor about the North-East Spur is that it is perfectly sheltered from the westerlies by the main North Ridge. Otherwise the type of work which we had to do in bad weather would have been impossible.

After climbing the steep gully and the deep snow slope, Kiran's party established Camp III at a height of 20,670 feet (6,300 metres) on the afternoon of April 26. Kiran described the site of Camp III as an 'oasis in the vertical hell of ice'. The site was on a hanging glacier on the Twins Glacier side of the ridge; the only place where three or four tents could be pitched. Luckily the climbers could not know that the camp was on a hanging glacier or we would not have been able to sleep properly there.

Till April 8 our progress had been very fast, almost too good to be true. We had overcome the Ice Fall. We had broken the defences of the treacherous south face leading to the crest of the North-East Spur, not at one but at two places. At that stage I had had no doubt that we could establish Camp III by April 10. The tragedy had however put us back by 16 days.

Kanchenjunga does not give you much time. Even under normal conditions, it is a race against the monsoons. And so far we were virtual non-starters to say the least. People in Delhi must have been very perturbed at the apparently slow rate of our progress. So when 16 days after setting up Camp II we established Camp III, it was a cause for rejoicing. We received a special congratulatory signal from the Chief of Army, General T.N. Raina, MVC, and Vice-Chief Lt-General O.P. Malhotra, PVSM. Though we had had a taste of the North-East Spur's terrifying defences, some people are incorrigible optimists: I am one of those and sent back a signal: "It may be possible to force open a route over the dangerous and difficult portion of the ridge in two or three days' time." A rude shock awaited me. Had I known then that it would take us another 16 days to Camp IV, I am not sure if we could have kept up the effort, since I wanted the team to be off the Spur much before the onset of the monsoons.

11

Taming
the North-East Spur

Normally to gain a thousand vertical feet at the altitude at which we were operating should not take more than two to three hours. On the North-East Spur of Kanchenjunga, it took us 16 days. The following passage, written by Allwein, a member of Paul Bauer's expedition, gives a vivid idea of the difficult terrain we had to negotiate:

"On September 23rd we had got as far as the fourth pinnacle, and for a while we stood there completely at a loss. The ridge was vertical or overhanging, and both the right and the left faces were overhanging, too, but a narrow ledge roofed by great overhanging masses of rock led into a groove deep in the ice. Soon after that the strip ended under impracticable ice overhangs. The only thing we could do was to drive a vertical tunnel from the groove upwards. Kraus started work on the tunnel—he slipped into the groove and started on the roof with his ice-axe. The work was terribly hard and exhausting and after a while one had to adopt back and knee technique in the ever-widening chimney in order to reach the roof, and, as you hacked, the loosened snow and ice fell down into your face and over your shoulders whilst the melted snow water soaked into your clothes no matter how carefully you had done yourself up. During the first hour of this tunnel building I occupied myself on the narrow ledge, which was difficult to use, turning it into a quite comfortable path on which even the biggest rucksack could be carried easily. The work took all day, and when we returned to the camp at four in the afternoon the tunnel still wasn't finished."

Of this effort, Frank Smythe, the great British climber remarked:

"Such hard work as this has never before been accomplished at such an altitude. Its technique opens out an entirely new method of overcoming these terrific Himalayan ice ridges. Though only time will tell whether routes of this difficulty will ever lead to victory on the greater peaks of the Himalayas."

So this was the task before Kiran, Kura Ram and Norbu. They started to tackle this portion of the Spur on April 27, sinking knee-deep in the snow at every step. Right in front of them, a small snow ridge rose, fell and rose again. They decided to traverse it from the left, i.e. the Zemu side, but there was hardly enough space even to put a foot on. The overhang was so low that they could not stand up on the small ledge they had found. They then tried the Twins Glacier side which proved worse, so they went back to the Zemu side. While Kiran belayed, Norbu removed his rucksack and tried to crouch under the ice overhang. There was still no place. He retraced his steps, looked at Kiran asking if the belay was fast, and then with all his might, he started axing the ice. Within a quarter of an hour Norbu was sweating profusely, while Kiran standing at one spot and belaying him could feel his feet starting to get numb. After an hour's work, only a little chunk had come off. But this gave them a place to recline. They changed places and Kiran went to work. It took them 3 hours to make a way through the ice overhang which was only 15 feet long. The weather turned bad as it usually did in the early afternoons, but they continued their labour in the wilderness of towers and chasms: removing snow, hacking steps, hammering pitons, tying ropes and all the time struggling to retain their balance on the sheer slope. Gradually, their sweat-soaked clothes grew soggy with cold and they called it a day. Five hours of back-breaking labour had yielded only a measly 50 feet.

Next day Kiran's party was luckier and they gained another 100 vertical feet. They reported that evening, "We have made a further progress of 500 feet, mostly horizontal, on the ridge." They were still following the Zemu side of the Spur. Then they hit mushroom-shaped formations of Neve snow. This is perhaps peculiar only to this area in the Himalayas, and is caused by a thawing and freezing process on the leeward side of the North-East Spur. Higher up, where the westerlies are active, the snow and ice conditions are normal. This snow was harder to negotiate and had to be continually hacked away. They had to cross one rib after another of such mushrooms and made agonizingly slow progress. Then, abruptly their way on the Zemu side ended in a sheer drop of hundreds of feet and further progress from this side became impossible. They had to switch over to the Twins Glacier side. They found a small opening in the snow and after two hours of hard labour, managed to dig a 12-foot long tunnel. Having fixed a rope in the tunnel, they could barely wriggle through after removing their rucksacks, and then pulled their rucksacks after them with the help of another rope. The tunnel opened into a rough crevasse, which brought them back to the Zemu side of the ridge. Thus far, in all they had fixed 500 feet of rope since Camp III. On the third day they gained another 200 feet before the weather turned bad. They had now been operating at about 21,000 feet for four days and Kura Ram

The Nandi Tower before Camp IV.

Coming down from Camp IV.

98

was already feeling the effects of the altitude. His appetite had completely vanished. He told me later, "Everything is fine except that I can't eat, and if I don't eat, I can't work."

Norbu and Kura Ram came down, while Kiran stayed on to show the route to Pushkar's rope who were to start working on the ridge for the first time. Pushkar was still not feeling well and needed to rest for another day. But I pushed up Gurcharan and Nirmal anyway. On April 30, Kiran took Nirmal and Gurcharan to his party's high point on the ridge. From Camp I, we could see them most of the time, except when they had to cross over to the Twins Glacier side of the ridge, or were in the tunnel. On May 1, Kiran came down to Base and Pushkar finally went up to Camp III. The same day, Nirmal and Gurcharan had started out on their own but they could find no sign of the tunnel. After a long search they realized that the tunnel must have collapsed. It took them a whole day to retrieve the rope that had been fixed in the tunnel, and re-make the route before bad weather forced them back to the camp.

That evening, a terrible blizzard struck all camps. Camp III was the worst hit. The tent was torn and filled with snow and the occupants had a tough time holding the tent down lest it be blown off. They tugged the torn side of the tent under their mattresses and grimly sat on it. Snow kept piling upon the tent and made the tent heavier, thereby reducing the chances of its being swept away. It was Pushkar's first night on the North-East Spur and Kanchenjunga seemed to be greeting him with all its fury. When they got out of the tent next morning, a white mantle of snow covered everything around them. During the long night they had given up all hopes of finding any stores that had been kept out. Luckily for them, however, the stores had been buried by the snow before the gale could get at them and no great damage was caused except that Kiran's rucksack had been blown away.

This was the fourth rucksack Kiran had managed to lose. He had jettisoned his original one when he had tried to disentangle Sukhvinder's body. Later, when Kura Ram had reached the spot, they had had to throw away Sukhvinder's rucksack to free his body off the rope. He had lent his spare one to Kura Ram which was left at our old Camp II. Kiran had then borrowed Prem's frameless rucksack and left it behind at Camp III when he came down to Base. Feeling very sheepish, he apologized to Prem first thing next morning but his credibility had sunk very low and no one was prepared to lend him another rucksack! He finally asked me. I could hardly refuse my brother. But all of us often pulled his leg about this.

In the evening, Pushkar came on the wireless and told me he was not feeling well. I consented to his coming down. When he reached Camp I, he came straight into my tent, "I have to go down," he pleaded and showed me a letter written by his Guru asking him to pray in a *gompa* before he started climbing. He had had no chance to do so as he had led the advance party to establish the Base Camp. This was the first time he had not obeyed his Guru and was convinced that all our troubles and the bad weather were due to this lapse of his. Pushkar had done a good job of opening the Base Camp and a route on the treacherous south face of the North-East Spur. I understood the state of his mind and let him rush down to Lachen.

Even the bravest of men becomes quite sensitive about his beliefs, feelings and duties during moments of great stress. This happens with everyone; it happened with us also. For instance, Kiran, while working on the ridge, sent a message to his wife to write to him "lest you have to repent later". Similarly, when on the ridge for the third time, I suddenly realized that I had not even written my will. So I quickly wrote one and kept it with all proper markings.

In a way I was relieved that Pushkar had come down. A man leading on North-East Spur should not have anything preying on his mind. This would not only endanger his own life but also of others working with him. Pushkar went down to Lachen, covering four stages in a day, and returned after a week. The trip made such a difference in him that he worked with renewed vigour and later went on to establish Camp VI.

But Pushkar's absence from the lead slowed down our push. Gurcharan and Nirmal felt that there ought to be at least three men on the rope, so that even if one of them slipped, the other two would be able to hold him. Also, they were facing highly adverse weather. However, they were still able to fix another 200 feet of rope by May 4, when they were relieved by Prem and N.D. It was thus not till May 5, with Prem back in the lead, that we regained our momentum.

I also went to Camp III with Prem and N.D., mainly to shoot some movie and still pictures of the route. Enroute we spent a night at Camp II. Climbers staying at Camp II often anchored themselves with a rope tied to a boulder so that they would not fall off the icy cliff. It was the most cramped camping site on the mountain. The gully beyond Camp II had a nearly 70 degree slope. A rope had been fixed but some stretches were so long that in the event the rope broke, there would be very little chance of survival. We fixed a second rope at this spot some time later.

The route first went left, then turned sharply to the right. On top of the gully, I could see a dangerous looking mushroom. I speculated what would happen if it broke. As the day warmed up, the snow plastered over the ice got loosened and slid down. No one could cross the gully without being covered by small flakes of snow. Prem was a hundred feet above me. As he climbed, small pieces of ice hurtled like pellets towards us. Fortunately, they were too small to do any real damage. On the upper part of the gully, where we could not keep to the side and had to stay in the centre, the rule was to move one at a time. The gully took us to

---

FACING: *Taming the Monster Tower*. OVERLEAF: *A panoramic view of Sikkim Himalayas from Camp III*. CENTRE-SPREAD LEFT: (Above) *Negotiating the steep icy cliffs between Camp III and Camp IV*. (Below) *The icy web enroute Camp IV*.

100

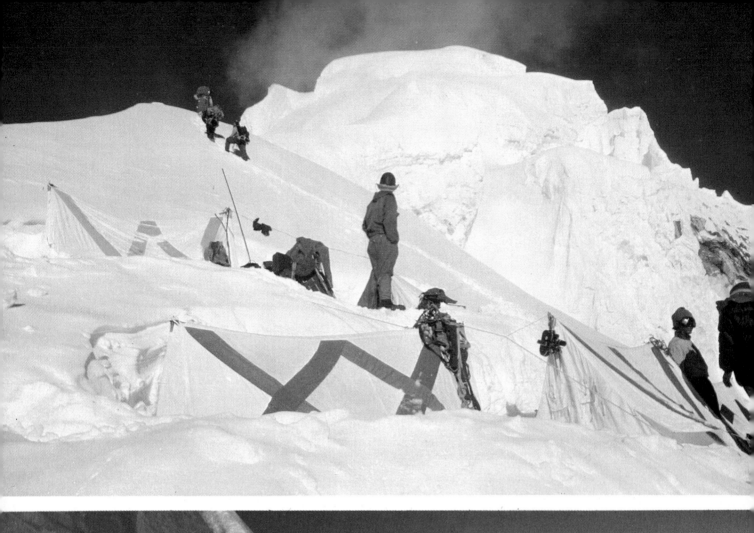

an almost vertical 10-foot high rock step where our fixed rope constantly chafed against the rock and there was obviously a great danger of its snapping due to friction. We used to keep an eagle's eye on it and the moment it frayed a little, we would put in a knot. Still it always gave me the creeps. The route then followed a rib which was connected to the main ridge by a thin snow ledge that fell away steeply on both sides.

From atop the ridge, we had a wonderful view of the snow-covered mountains all around. Behind us we could see the route we had taken; the spine-like ridge climbing up and the complete horizontal traverse on the sheer slope. The Twins Glacier side of the ridge looked more dangerous than the Zemu side. The Twins Peak and Sugar Loaf Peak looked deceptively close and towards the south-east lay Simvo's sheer, simmering walls of rock, glazed with ice. But Siniolchu did not appear as grand as it did from the Rest Camp area. In the distance we could see Chomalhari trailing its famous plume. From here I was also able to fully appreciate Prem and Kiran's feat of hacking a way over this dangerous ridge. Passing through this tricky maze, we reached Camp III which was pitched on a ledge which dropped away sheer on both sides. Even the slope we had climbed had at least a 50 degree angle. I saw the crevasse which had opened up on the Twins Glacier side of the ledge but our tents seemed pretty safe.

Ahead of us a huge tower barred our way like a monster. It was perhaps the last obstacle on the Spur but I could see no way to overcome it. In the afternoon the weather turned bad and we retired to our tents. Gurcharan complained of stomach-ache but it was nothing very serious. I was happy to have Prem in the lead again and felt things would now move faster. At that stage, we both thought that we ought to consider ourselves lucky if we could reach the German high point; the summit seemed a far cry. All through the night, a strong wind thrashed at our tent making it flap about wildly. At first we remained tensely awake, fearing that the wind might blow us away, but gradually we relaxed and drifted off to sleep.

The next day I had planned to see the high point reached by Gurcharan and Nirmal. I also wanted to shoot some cine films and then return to Camp I, for as yet Camp III did not have enough supplies for all of us. But in the morning the weather was still foul. We should have expected it after the previous night's strong wind. In that weather it was out of the question for me to go photographing and I decided to go down. Prem advised me against it, especially since even the sherpas from Camp I had decided not to do a carry that day. But we were three extra persons at Camp III not doing any useful work, and I felt that progress on the mountain would suffer if we stayed on. I asked Gyalzen if he would like

CENTRE-SPREAD RIGHT: *Major Prem Chand at Camp IV with the south face of the Twins Peak in the background.* OVERLEAF LEFT: (Above) *A ferry setting off from Camp IV* (Below) *Camp V at 23,720 feet.* OVERLEAF RIGHT: (Above) *The track leading up from Camp V and the summit in the background.* (Below) *On way to Camp VI.* FACING: (Above) *A view towards Bhutan Himalayas from the North-East Spur.* (Below) *The arete culminating at the highest point of the Spur.*

109

to come with me and he promptly agreed. Gyalzen was the most likeable sherpa on the mountain, and the smartest. He was soft-spoken and could speak better English than the other sherpas. He was also a good climber and personally, I liked him the best of the lot. Prem again tried to dissuade me but I felt it would be simple for us to descend on the familiar route. Prem himself was going up. "I'm just going to see what they have done," he said and was off, without even waiting for his companion. We started our downward journey at 8 a.m.

About a foot of snow had fallen during the night and wiped out our tracks. So the first problem was to dig out the fixed rope just below Camp III. Gyalzen was in the lead followed by Gonchuk, and I brought up the rear. We sank knee-deep in the fresh snow but with the help of the fixed rope we pushed on. We descended a steep slope, crossed over a deep furrow and came to a traverse. Another steep gully followed and then a 20-foot long traverse on a 70-degree slope. Before starting on the traverse I absently fixed my jumar to the rope. About half-way on the traverse the snow under my feet suddenly gave way and I was flung off the slope. Luckily my fall was arrested as the rope at my waist stretched taut. At first I thought it was all over for me. Then I calmed down and took stock of the situation. Luckily I had not hit my head on a rock. Still, I was hanging 16 feet below the track and could see the base of the cliffs where they met the Zemu Glacier, almost fifteen hundred feet below. Gyalzen and Gonchuk had by then descended another gully and were at least half an hour away. I shouted at them to stop but with the wind blowing furiously, it was a futile gesture. Slowly I realized that I would have to climb up to the track on my own.

The first thing I did was to stop looking down at the frightening fall below. Then I swung myself around until I faced the slope and at that moment it flashed through my mind that had the rope snapped, I would have been lying splattered on the snows far below. A cold chill ran through my body, but I again forced my mind away from such thoughts and concentrated on climbing back to safety. My absent-minded action of attaching my jumar to the fixed rope had helped reduce my fall by at least another 10 feet. I kicked my crampons into the ice to get some support and then tried to push the jumar up. But it had got stuck with the pressure of the fall and would not budge an inch. I tried to release it, but found it jammed with ice. For fifteen long, tortuous minutes I struggled with the jumar and thought of a similar accident that had claimed Harsha Bahuguna on Everest. How suddenly and simply one meets his end, I reflected. Though I was safe for the moment but the weather was becoming worse, reducing the chances of any rescue party to come to my aid. I did not have a knife to cut my jumar loose, and I almost broke my hands trying to release it. Finally in desperation, I cupped the jumar with my hands and blew on it in an effort to melt the ice that clogged it. At last it moved a little but then slipped back. The rope was so heavily covered with snow that the jumar would not hold. It was of no help. I gave up struggling with the jumar, twisted the rope around my wrists and then pulled myself up with all the strength

110

I could muster. It was now or never. Inching upwards, I struggled up to the four-inch wide truck. But only when I had completed the traverse did I feel safe and alive and made a resolve never again to use a jumar on the traverses.

After crossing the next gully, I saw Gyalzen and Gonchuk going ahead. They were naturally unaware of what had happened to me. I thought it best not to tell them and cause unnecessary worry. I caught up with them on the steep gully just above Camp II. I was curious to see how this gully behaved after receiving fresh snowfall. Gyalzen was the first to descend. The moment he stepped onto the snow it slid, but it also brought more snow upon him and he was covered upto his waist but he ploughed through it. When it was my turn I thought that most of the snow would have been driven down, but fresh snow continued to come down from the top. I was at times covered upto my chest, and kept taking small hops to press it under my feet. I realized the problem the Germans must have faced when they came down this ridge with 6 feet of fresh snow.

While going up I had sworn that I would never again stay at Camp II. But the weather was bad, I was tired and even this camp looked quite inviting. Gyalzen made some delicious salt tea. We munched some biscuits and had a very comfortable night. In the morning, to our dismay, I found Gonchuk had turned snow-blind; his eyes were swollen and red, and pained acutely. Despite this, he climbed down slowly to Camp I.

From Camp I, I sent up Norbu to fix an extra rope on two traverses. I had to tell him of the accident I had met. He in turn informed me that he too had fallen at the same place. Norbu not only fixed the extra rope but also tied it to an extra piton so that it was taut. This made the pitch far more secure. More bad news awaited me at Camp I, Dr Cruz reported that Jawahar had contracted some gall-bladder trouble and had to be evacuated. My team was being cut down day by day but there was nothing I could do about it. Jawahar was evacuated soon after and that was the end of the expedition for him.

Meanwhile up at Camp III, Prem and N.D. helped by Gurcharan and Nirmal on first two days, were cutting out some sort of a route in the ice, sometimes on the Zemu side of the Spur and, at others, on the Twins side. We could see them at work from Camp I. Bad weather plagued us daily but the work on the mountain continued. On the morning of May 8, we saw two specks reach the bottom of the Monster Tower. They turned left, and then went back. Then we saw one of them struggling up the leaning tower. It was a wonder to see how he could cling to the overhanging slope: it looked impossibly steep and smooth. However, after two hours, they had scaled the tower and we saw one of them standing on the top. A little later he was joined by the second speck. The first one then disappeared on to the left and came back after quite some time. Then they both descended. I hoped this would be our last major obstacle for we had no time now to tackle another. We could see more towers from Camp I but I had a notion that we would find easier going around them.

On the next day, i.e. May 9, Prem and his party went up again and by 10 a.m. they had crossed the Monster Tower and disappeared behind it. Late in the evening, we saw them on the eastern face of the last conical tower and I knew they must have found easier ground, otherwise they could not have reached that far so quickly. Then the clouds concealed them from our view. With growing impatience, we waited for the wireless call scheduled for 4 p.m. Had they finally found the key to the North-East Spur? Time dragged on very slowly and finally Prem's voice crackled over the air:

"Hello Camp III, report signal."

"How are you, Prem?" I asked.

"Exhausted," he replied.

"How did you fare?" I was biting my nails now. All our hopes depended on what Prem said next.

"The Spur is over. We are at the snow-field."

"What did you say? Please repeat that."

He repeated that they had negotiated the Spur and hit the normal slopes. After congratulating him I rushed out of my tent and shouted like a mad man. "The Spur is over! The Spur is done!!" and went to every tent to give them the glad tidings. Soon everybody was dancing with joy. The sherpas too joined us. This was the day I had been waiting for. We had overcome the most difficult part of the mountain. I was so excited that I could not sleep that night.

After climbing the Monster Tower, Prem and N.D. had found a broad ledge. This ledge ended abruptly after about 400 yards and they had gone back to the crest of the ridge again. This seemed the last tower of the North-East Spur but there appeared no way to skirt it. So Prem had tackled it head-on. It took him hours of cutting steps, clawing grimly with crampons, fixing pitons and aluminium bars. On the top of the tower there was a great overhang which they tension-climbed. After that, only a thin ridge separated them from the beckoning, easy slopes. It was tricky but seemed almost a cake-walk after their struggle with the tower. They returned to Camp III completely exhausted.

Peak 7780 on the Eastern Ridge of Kanchenjunga as seen from Camp I.

12

The Higher Slopes

Camp IV to Camp VI

Our joy at the opening of the route to Camp IV was, however, extremely short-lived. The next day, i.e. May 10, the expedition suffered another major setback. While the advance parties had been at work to overcome the defences of the Spur, we had created a dump of stores near the Crampon Point. Even inexperienced porters could bring up loads from Advance Base to this point without crampons. These loads were then transported to higher camps by sherpas and team members, as and when required. In the past few days, while we had been concentrating our attention on opening and stocking the higher camps on the Spur, loads had piled up at this dump. It was only when our Food Officer, Dr Cruz warned that there would be no food or tea the next day did we send a party to bring up some of the stuff.

Within two hours they were back. Paul Jaur of Manali, who was the first to arrive, threw down his empty rucksack and muttered, "All gone, all gone. Thank God, we were not there." Then, calming down, he told us that all the stores had been buried by a very big ice avalanche and the dump at the Crampon Point had disappeared! Jai Bahuguna and Dr Cruz went down with some sherpas to take stock of the situation. Returning late in the evening, they reported: "We could hardly recognize the place. The entire dump has been wiped out." They could find only one oxygen bottle, at the foot of the avalanche, which had miraculously not leaked. The avalanche had peeled off the glacier overhang next to the Rock Island. All along I had been scared of this overhang and finally it

113

had shown its teeth. Normally we avoided moving in the Ice Fall after 10 a.m. because of the danger of such an avalanche, but this one had come early in the morning.

I thanked our lucky stars that no one had been hurt. Our situation was serious. All the rations we had at Camp I had to be sent up the next day. We were already running against time and only now had we seen a ray of hope of getting to the summit. I did not want to spoil our chances in any way. So we decided to live on hard rations that day and not touch the food intended for the higher camps. We explained the problem to the sherpas and they too willingly agreed to our decision. We were deeply touched by their support. There was nothing to do except wait for more stores to come up from the Base Camp. Dr Sen, who was handling the logistics at Advance Base, made people carry double loads by paying four times the normal wages in an effort to quickly make up for the loss caused by the avalanche.

That evening for the first time, I noticed thin, feathery, cirrus clouds forming in the distance. Such clouds are the sure forerunners of the approaching bad weather. Bad weather struck soon after and we had a foot of snow during the night. The weather took twenty-four hours to clear and no carries from Advance Base were possible during this period. This was the only day during the entire expedition, when no work at all could be done. However, porters brought up rations to the Crampon Point from the Advance Base Camp, and we picked these up. Meanwhile Kiran, Norbu, Kura Ram and Khushal had replaced Prem's party in the lead and established Camp IV at a height of 21,750 feet (6,630 metres) on May 12. After the snowfall, Kiran's party made a daring probe. Climbing the steep slopes they would sink thigh-deep in the snow. Each step was a struggle and they had a terrible time beating out a track, yet they gained an amazing 1,000 vertical feet that day. It was great going under extremely difficult conditions.

After this pitch they hit the normal climbing slopes—no more of the ridge, no more towers, no more mushrooms. But then there were soft snow and strong winds which gave the climbers a very rough time. Every day the track would be obliterated; every day it had to be remade. The approaching monsoons caused another growing worry. After 10 a.m., clouds would gather and lay an impenetrable white curtain over the mountain, causing white-out conditions and reducing the visibility almost to nil. The marker flags could not be seen even from a distance of 10 yards. Twice our ferry parties had to return from the Monster Tower for they could not make out the route beyond.

Clearly we needed many more marker flags but all the remaining ones lay buried under the debris of the avalanche. We rushed a man down to Poke to bring up thin bamboos which could be used as markers. Cloth for the flags was no problem since many members had coloured underwear! Then on May 12, the sherpas protested that they would not go up the ridge as the daily evening snowfall presented continuing danger of avalanches. All at once, the expedition seemed to be grinding to a halt. I was however, convinced that there was no chance of a big avalanche as the slope was too steep, and with the fixed rope in place there was no danger of a climber being swept off it. In order to convince the porters I decided to take a party through myself.

The morning of the carry, I somehow got delayed and started half-an-hour after the main party, hoping to catch up with them fairly quickly. All went well till I reached the avalanche cone below the gully, where the south face of the Spur meets the Zemu Glacier. At this point, the tracks made by the party which had just gone up were nowhere to be seen, nor were there any signs of the fixed rope. I tried to climb the cone but kept sinking hip-deep in the soft avalanche snow. It was almost impossible to go on, but to turn back would have had a demoralizing effect on the sherpas. I took off my load, two oxygen bottles on a carrier, and started beating the snow in front of me. Then with the help of the load, I pulled myself up and beat the ground under my feet. It was hard work, my progress was painfully slow. I wished I had started up with the main party, and then there had been 8 people to make a track.

I wondered how so much snow could have accumulated in half-an-hour and at once realized that more avalanches would come once the rocks got warmed by the sun. Keeping close to the rocks for safety, I had barely climbed about 15 yards, when I heard the unmistakable rumble of an approaching avalanche from above, and before I could take shelter among the rocks a large mass of snow engulfed me. Fortunately, my feet were firmly anchored in the soft snow and I was able to retain my balance. I was not much worried by the snow but dreaded the possibility of some stones following in its wake. Luckily none came. The avalanche lasted for about 15 seconds and when it was over, I found myself buried waist-deep in the snow. The loose powdery stuff had also got under my collar. I took off my goggles, cleaned them out and shook the upper half of my body free of it. Then I dug out my rucksack which had been buried and slowly pulled myself

The route from Camp V to Camp VI.

out of the snow and resumed climbing.

This experience, however, convinced me that ferries could continue even during bad weather and after about a foot of fresh snow. The sheerness of the Spur which had posed severe problems earlier, now proved a big boon as the steep slopes were secure from the dangers of avalanches. I reached Camp II, dumped my load and returned late in the evening, completely spent. But the purpose had been served. Thereafter, no sherpa ever missed a ferry because of fresh snow. Many of them experienced similar avalanches but the fixed rope was enough to save them from being swept off the slope. This of course required that the fixed rope be kept completely free of snow since it was the crucial life-line for anyone caught in an avalanche. I also announced an extra bonus of a hundred rupees for every load carried from Camp III to Camp IV and the ferries continued regularly. We still had a chance on the mountain.

On the third day of work between Camp IV and Camp V, Kiran came down with diarrhoea, perhaps as a result of over-eating. On account of lack of oxygen at high altitudes, the digestive system is affected and one can digest very little. So, unless the diet is reduced, undigested food ferments in the stomach. Hundreds of climbers have suffered from overlooking this factor and been led into believing it was some infection. Kura Ram was also ill, so Norbu went up alone to the high point of the previous day and single-handedly fixed another 300 feet of rope. It was a stunning achievement but I pulled him up for climbing alone on such a terrain. I did not want any more accidents on the mountain.

The next day, all of them went up and made trail almost to Camp V. By now we had enough stores at Camp IV to start stocking up Camp V. So the next day I sent up Gurcharan, Nirmal and Wangyal for this purpose. They had a difficult time beating out the track opened earlier by Kiran's party. Since at this altitude, we had started encountering the westerlies that caused snow drifts and covered up the tracks. In the evening, Gurcharan told me over the wireless, "It is impossible to carry the camp up in one day." This was the longest haul between any two camps, the difference in altitude between Camp IV and Camp V being nearly 2,000 feet (600 metres). They first set up a temporary intermediate camp and on May 19, finally established Camp V at a height of 23,720 feet (7,230 metres).

Meanwhile, Kiran's party was coming down. Just below Camp IV, they were caught in a total white-out and got lost in the snow-field above the Monster Tower. They could see no markers and there were no visible tracks to follow. After stumbling around for two hours, one of them accidentally chanced on the fixed rope. This was to prove a tough problem and a constant worry from now on. It was not possible to fix ropes on the entire route. And the seven markers

FACING: (Above) *Colonel Kumar giving the National Flag to the summit party.*
(Below) *Ominous signs of the approaching monsoon contesting the race to the summit.*

116

that had been put were not enough. As we kept putting additional markers on the route, the situation improved a little. I also charged Dorje and Angchuk at Camp III to keep the route to Camp IV in good shape, and also escort all upgoing ferries. This part of the route had now become the crux of the entire climb, and their job was to ensure that the ferries operated smoothly and without any hitch to maintain our build-up for the summit. Dorje and Angchuk did an excellent job here and our pace higher up on the mountain was never slowed down due to any logistical bottleneck.

Pushkar returned from Lachen after offering his prayers in the *gompa* there. He told us that the Darjeeling mountaineering circles had come to the conclusion that it was too late for us to reach the summit since the monsoons were nearly upon us. Disregarding all such predictions, I pushed Pushkar and Angchuk straight up to Camp V, and told them to open the route to Camp VI. For the first two days they could not make any progress due to bad weather but once they got going, they discovered an easy and short route. The only problem was that as they got higher, the influence of the westerlies grew stronger. They climbed a saddle between two humps and then followed the crest of the ridge, until it ended at Camp VI. I had all along wanted Camp VI to be in the Col, just below the North Ridge, and so when Pushkar sent a message that they had reached the Col, I was thrilled. Later it turned out that Camp VI had actually been established not at the Col but just before a knife-edge arete at an altitude of 25,030 feet (7,630 metres).

The date was May 24 and by my reckoning, the monsoon now only a week away. Time was running out as the Darjeeling mountaineers had said, but on the other hand our pace had certainly quickened. It had taken us 17 days after established Camp II to open up Camp III, and another 16 agonizing ones before we could set up Camp IV. Once having overcome the extreme severity of the North-East Spur, we had set up Camp V and VI in another fortnight, climbing another 3,280 feet in the process. Our morale was high and everyone was doing his bit cheerfully and confidently. We seemed to have got over the shock of Sukhvinder's death and the early depletion of our team. We all were now full of confidence in our ability to get to the top.

Could we accelerate our progress some more or did Kanchenjunga yet hold some obstacles on its higher slopes that would require more time to overcome than we had? I thought of the ice-wall that guarded our approach to the North Ridge. Nearly half a century ago, the Germans too had mastered the Spur but had their efforts ground to a halt by its cracked wind-slabs. In the silence of the evening I looked up towards the summit, but it was blanketed in an impenetrable white-out.

OVERLEAF: *Climbing on the North Ridge to Camp VII with the summit in the background.* FACING: (Above) *Naik N.D. Sherpa at Camp VII.* (Below) *The wind-eroded western flank of the North Ridge.*

13

The North Ridge

I had started thinking about the possible composition of the summit parties as soon as Camp IV had been established. For any leader, this is a very unpleasant decision to make. If I could, I would always have all the members getting to the summit together, but logistic problems on a high mountain obviously do not allow such an easy solution. Nevertheless, it is always my endeavour to put as many members on top as possible. On Everest in 1965, we had nine reaching the top, and on Chomalhari in 1973, I had been able to send five to the summit. On Kanchenjunga too, I had always planned on putting at least two parties on the summit.

It is at this juncture in the expedition that the leader has to be dispassionate and objective about the performance and ambitions of the members, some of whom are always bound to feel hurt when their desires are found to be against the dictates of the objective demands. I consoled myself by the fact that in the ultimate analysis, a major climb is always a team affair.

There are many points to be considered in selecting a summit team. First, the summiteers should obviously be in excellent physical condition. There have been many instances of climbers working themselves to early exhaustion for the sake of the expedition and being physically unfit for the final push to the summit. A leader normally tries to equally distribute difficult pitches among the members, but for any number of reasons it is not always possible to do so. Thereafter, the leader has to be fair to those who have worked harder and taken more risks than the others though under some circumstances such people may have to be over-looked in the larger interests of the expedition.

The third major factor to my mind is that the potential summiteers should have faith in each other's capabilities. Such confidence is absolutely essential, as very often during the final attempt, a time comes when one of the climbers may feel defeated, but take heart from his companion's strength and spirit. Next, there must be temperamental compatibility among the summiteers. Due to a lack of oxygen, climbers are prone to be highly irritable at high altitude and even small problems are magnified out of all proportions. Last but not the least, I wanted the summit party to have a balanced mix of both the non-commissioned and commissioned officers since both were in equal numbers in the expedition. This would also ensure that at least one of the summiteers would know of the functioning of the oxygen equipment.

Prem and N.D. eminently fulfilled all these considerations and virtually select-ed themselves for the first summit party. Prem was perfectly fit but N.D. had just had an attack of high altitude piles and had lost a lot of blood. In fact, at one time the doctors had wanted him evacuated but Dr Sen now assured me that N.D. had fully recovered. There was of course a possibility of his piles erupting again at a higher altitude, but I decided to run the risk in view of the excellent combi-nation he made with Prem. I did however, take the precaution of having a reserve at hand to replace N.D. at any stage.

Once the first summit party was announced, I took Prem and N.D. off the mountain and sent them down to the Base Camp, where Dr Sen almost comple-tely overhauled them by giving them all types of injections to make up for the deficiencies caused by a long stay at high altitude. To support the first summit party, and to make the second attempt, I selected Kiran and Norbu. As our second summit party, theirs would be a hard task. These two were also taken off the mountain as soon as the route to Camp V had been opened. The itinerary of these two teams had then to be carefully worked out to ensure that they did not spend too much time at high altitude before the actual summit attempts and suffer from deterioration of body cells causing unnecessary physical weakness.

As the summit parties moved up after their stay at the Base Camp, hectic activity was going on at all camps. At Base, sick people were convalescing. Young girls carried double loads to the Advance Base Camp to keep the higher camps adequately stocked. Their menfolk had shifted to Advance Base and we were now paying them double wages. The Advance Base Camp had become a busy ad-ministrative centre. Some boys from the Ladakh Scouts who had not been able to get fully acclimatized, were ferrying loads from the Advance Base to the Cramp-on Point dump. Though they had not been able to adjust to the heights, they re-tained their sense of humour and high spirits.

On one occasion, they had brought a pretty Lachen girl through the Ice Fall to Camp I. That night there was no vacant tent there except mine. They hesitated for some time but then unanimously agreed that the extraordinary beauty of the young lady deserved an extraordinary status. So she was put up in the leader's tent for the night!

With so much activity going on, the Ice Fall had become a thoroughfare and Camp I the nerve-centre of the climb. Surjit, who had now taken over from Capt Dr Cruz the responsibility of keeping the ferries moving up, started his day at five in the morning. Even though weather was most of the time bad, ferry after ferry went up from Camp I with clock-like regularity. There were plenty of other jobs to be done for anyone who could not go higher. The men were utilized to bring up stores from the Crampon Point dump. These people made two or three trips every day and thus played an important part in the final logistic build-up. Camp I itself, was almost always short of food, for whatever came up from Advance Base was pushed up to higher camps. There were of course the occasional blizzards, but these were not a cause of any great alarm; life at Camp I was generally pretty comfortable.

Once when a helicopter came to evacuate Jawahar, who had contracted frost-bite, I asked Surjit to go down to Base Camp and try to persuade the pilot to fly close to the Spur as we wanted to shoot some aerial pictures. Despite a bad ankle, Surjit reached Base in record time—twice as fast as I would have made it—and then took the pictures we wanted. Upon returning, he talked of some unclimbable gap ahead of the North-East Spur, and also told us how dangerously Camp III was located on an overhanging glacier. We gratefully took the pictures from him but ignored his bad news, for it was too late to do anything about it. I was astonished by Surjit's performance, more so since he had a hurt ankle, and came to know only later that the doctor had given him some pain-killing injections, and he had run all the way to make sure that he got to Base Camp before the effect of the medicine wore off!

Meanwhile, Camp II had become nearly redundant. People preferred to go straight to Camp III and return from there straight to Camp I, for Camp II was an awful place to stay in. However, it was reassuring to know it was there in case of an emergency. Ferrying between Camp I and Camp III had lost its terrors. Not that the route had become any less dangerous but we had been going over it so often by now that we had become immune to the dangers. However, people going up for the first time still trembled at the first sight of the Spur. Once on my way up, I found one of the boys sitting helplessly on the knife-edge section of the Spur with steep vertical drops on either side. He was immobilized with fright. Upon seeing me, he mustered courage and got across. I sympathized with him since most of us had encountered somewhat similar feelings when we had gone up for the first time.

When I was going up this route with the summit party, I was very concerned to discover that the pitons and the aluminium bars on the fixed ropes would hold firm in the morning but become dangerously loose in the afternoon. I immediately

124

arranged a constant watch on these fixed ropes. Just above Camp II, there was a large overhanging mushroom of Neve snow atop the gully. It had worried us throughout the expedition but had fortunately held till now.

One day however, when Wangyal, one of our finest high-altitude porters, was returning after carrying a load to Camp III, he heard a cracking sound. Looking up, he found that a large portion of the mushroom had broken off and was toppling straight down upon him. Wangyal was in the middle of the gully and exactly in line of the mushroom's fall. Like lightning he leapt and gripped the fixed rope and was able to get out of harm's way. A piece of the falling debris hit the frame of his rucksack and bent it almost double, but Wangyal was saved. It was a very lucky escape indeed. Though understandably shaken, Wangyal did not mention this upon his return lest it frighten the others. I was very moved by his gesture. We had hired these sherpas for their muscles but they, in turn, had put their hearts into our venture. No leader could ask for more.

At Camp III, Dr Cruz not only gave medical aid but also supervised the carries to higher camps. Though it was Dr Cruz's first major expedition, he performed like a seasoned mountaineer. Once, when there was an emergency request for some kerosene oil from Camp IV and no sherpas were available, he took up the load himself without any hesitation. At Camp IV, young Jai Bahuguna held the fort. He had earlier not been able to acclimatize and had fallen so sick that he had had to be removed to the Base Camp. I had lost all hopes of his recovering in time, but the impending summit attempts had put new life into him and he was soon back and escorting ferry after ferry from Camp IV to Camp V. During

Camp VI at height 25,030 feet.

the later stages of the expedition, when one of the Ladakhi boys fell ill on the route, Jai carried the sick climber's load in addition to his own. Unfortunately, he too contracted frost-bite during the final stage, and had to be evacuated. His place was taken over by Dr Cruz who was in turn relieved at Camp III by Dr Sen.

I left Camp I with the first summit party on May 22 and stayed the night at Camp III, reaching Camp IV on May 23. About the route between Camp III and Camp IV, I wrote in my diary, "The route starts along the left side of ridge with a crawl under an ice overhang and then passes through a very interesting jungle of ice mushrooms. One of these we christened 'Elephant' for it very much resembled this huge animal. We had to cross it by straddling over it. Then we came to the 'Camel' and had to pass under its legs. There is then a tricky spot where the ridge falls sheer on both sides and the aluminium bar is so loose that if one were not to press down on one's rope, the bar could jump out and throw one off. At two or three places we had to crawl through ice tunnels. One has the choice of going either leg-first or head-first."

I was thrilled when we reached the base of the Monster Tower. I had been looking at it through my binoculars for almost a month and I knew every crack,

The Col at the junction of North-East Spur and the North Ridge.

every furrow in it. As I jumared up the fixed rope I silently marvelled at Prem for having made a route over this obstacle. At the top of the tower, I was amazed to find a flat plateau about 500 yards long. Thereafter, we had to climb the ridge again. The last tower, which was conical in shape, was about 30 feet tall and supported a fairly large overhang at the top. We had really to struggle to reach its top. The sherpas invariably took off their loads before climbing up this tower, and then pulled the loads with a rope after them. This could have been avoided if we had been able to use an aluminium ladder but the problem was of getting one up here.

There was a flat platform on the top of the tower with a thin ridge connecting it to the wide main slopes ahead. About 10 feet of this thin ridge was barely a foot wide with almost perpendicular drops on both the sides. An aluminium bar had been fixed in the centre of this pitch and to cross it, one had to sit down, unlatch the karabiner from one rope and put it on the second, and so on. I was full of appreciation for the Ladakhi boys and sherpas who had been crossing it with heavy loads, day in and day out. Camp IV was situated on the side of a hump and two terraces had been made for our tents. The camp site offered a beautiful view on three sides. The view of Chomalhari was better than before, especially in the early mornings.

On May 25, we moved up from Camp IV to Camp V. It took us 6 hours of continuous slogging over the wide snow fields to get there. This camp was situated below the vertical ice-wall of a large hump. We had barely reached the camp, when I was surprised to find Ila Tashi, our Sherpa Sirdar, and six other sherpas coming down from Camp VI. I had selected these seven to carry up our Camp VII in support of the summit party and they had moved up from the Base a day ahead of us. They were tough and acclimatized and I had had no doubts that they would be able to make the carry to Camp VII. However, upon reaching Camp VI, they had encountered a half-mile long ice arete which had to be negotiated to get to Camp VII. They sized up the obstacle and came to the conclusion that it would take us at least 10 days to make a route across. Aware that the monsoons were to hit the area in about 5 days, they thought that there was no point in their staying at Camp VI any longer and had decided to return to Base Camp on their own.

Now at Camp V, Ila Tashi came into my tent with tears in his eyes to bid me good-bye. I could read his innermost thoughts; he seemed to be saying, "Alas, three months of risks taken and a life lost has come to nought. There is no hope, now you'd better call it off." I tried to persuade him to stay on a little longer but they had made up their minds and left for their downwards journey to Base.

From Camp V, the summit seemed finally within our reach, but the going away of the sherpas diminished our hopes. I sat in the tent wondering whether we would now be able to support the summit party to the last camp even if we could negotiate the arete in time. The bare minimum requirements of Camp VII would be two sleeping bags, one tent, two air mattresses, a stove, some food, six bottles of oxygen, each weighing nearly 15 lb, two regulators and other accessories for the oxygen equipment, two cameras, some fixed rope, a few ice and rock pitons and a wireless set, apart from the personal equipment of the climbers. By my estimate, a minimum of six sherpas would be required for such a carry from Camp VI to Camp VII. I had selected seven in case we needed a reserve, but now we had none. This was perhaps the biggest setback to our final effort.

My first night up in Camp V was not very pleasant. Through some miscalculation, there was one sleeping bag less than what we needed. Prem and all others offered me their sleeping bags but I refused. They all had a hard task ahead. So I put on a pair of down-trousers and my boots, and slept without a bag. I had a few sniffs of oxygen to make sure that my frost-bitten feet behaved. We were so tightly packed in the Swiss tent that no one could move and everyone slept in the position he adopted initially. Zangbo was next to me and snored like hell. But I was happy that he was so fit.

The next day, May 26, I decided to go up to Camp VI and see the dangerous arete which had turned back the sherpas. Surprisingly, even though we were quite high on the mountain, the day was not very cold. The sun hit us early and Gyalbo made some porridge for breakfast. As we were about to leave, a snow-slide started from the ridge and engulfed our camp. Luckily it was not very big and buried only half of a tent but we realized that it was a dangerous site for camping. Whenever there was a heavy snowfall, we would have to vacate the tent or face the risk of being buried alive. Though this particular slide had not done any material damage, it had covered the tracks leading to the top of the ridge, and the lead climbers had a terrible time ploughing through the snow. We climbed straight up to the ridge between the second and third humps. To overcome the second hump, a 100 feet of rope had been fixed and we jumared up. After that, we climbed on the Twins Glacier side, staying about 6 feet below the crest of the North-East Spur. It was easy going, but the altitude was now affecting us a lot and every step was a great effort. The weather was good and I shot a good length of a movie film.

Upon reaching Camp VI, I felt a bit unwell. After resting for half an hour in the only tent available, I borrowed an oxygen mask from Prem and went up with N.D. to see the knife-edge arete about fifty yards ahead. It was a stupendous sight; a half-mile-long wafer-thin ridge ending in a tooth. This was the obstacle that had made our sherpas return to the Base Camp. Though it did look dangerous but to me it seemed nothing compared with what we had already overcome on the North-East Spur. N.D. and Tashi Dorje had already started working on it and

FACING: (Above) *Naik N.D. Sherpa climbing the final lap to the summit.* (Below) *The summit with its western snow-field.* OVERLEAF: (Above) *Major Prem Chand on the summit.* (Below) *The tricolour planted 6 feet below the summit of Kanchenjunga.*

had fixed about 300 feet of rope. I went across the roped pitch. Maybe I was happy to find that the dire predictions of the sherpas were not true, or maybe I had been thinking and dreading it so much that in my mind it had assumed impossible proportions, but it was the most fascinating walk I have ever had in my mountaineering life. I wanted to press on further but N.D. pointed towards his boots and I saw he was not wearing crampons.

I stood there, within striking distance of the summit and ruminated for a long time. I was visualizing the disappointment of the Germans, who half a century earlier, had stood just a little further on the tooth point and looked despairingly at the face of the North Ridge, ultimately calling off their magnificent attempt.

I went to Camp VI and had a short consultation with Prem about our future plans. He was confident that he could reach the North Ridge in two days. His confidence was contagious and I returned to Camp V, tired but satisfied that the lead was in the best hands. Perhaps we could make the summit.

The next day Prem, N.D. and Dorje, who was now climbing extremely well after some initial set-backs, overcame the knife-edge arete. They fixed rope across its entire length and reached the highest point of the famous North-East Spur, and then descended to 'The Beautiful Col', as Prem had christened it. The Col was approximately two hundred yards long, flat as a football ground, and of about the same width as one. They then took on the face leading on to the North Ridge which had sent the Germans back.

On account of the action of the westerlies, this face gets heavy snow from the western face. This wind action causes wind slabs and such conditions are most conducive to avalanches. When the Germans had reached this point on the North-East Spur, they had noticed some windslabs cracking and they had decided not to take any chances. But Prem's party encountered very stable conditions and had little difficulty in negotiating it at the first attempt. With remarkable foresight, Prem had carried five bottles of oxygen, one small tent and some climbing equipment and dumped it on North Ridge. It was a great step forward. Prem had said he would be at the North Ridge in two days, but he had made it in one.

From the top of the face, Prem had his first good look at the North Ridge, which he had to follow to the summit. It came as a pleasant surprise; the mountain which was so sheer on its eastern side, had vast snow-fields on its west, and the ridge looked eminently negotiable. Towards the west, they could see the Everest group; towards the south rose the Twins; to our east Simvo and Siniolchu appeared mere dwarfs; and in the distance, Prem could see his own mountain, Chomalhari. He was exultant because he was now standing where no one had ever stood before.

OVERLEAF: (Above) *Point 8,500 on the traverse to south summit.* (Below) *Naik N.D. Sherpa on the summit.* FACING: (Above) *The west ridge of Kanchenjunga seen from the summit.* (Below) *The approaching monsoons.*

133

14

The Summit At Last

On May 28, Prem told me that he would like to set off for the summit the next morning without waiting any more for the arrival of the support party. He felt confident that he and N.D. stood a fairly good chance of success. But I was not at all in favour of going unprepared and thus risking our success. They needed a minimum of six oxygen bottles, four for use during the climb and two for use at night. These, and other essential equipment like tent, ropes, sleeping bags, mattresses, stove, food, etc, had yet to be sent up and just the two of them could not carry it all by themselves.

Besides the climbing equipment, the wireless set for the last camp had also yet to be sent up. A summit party without the means of communication with its rear lines runs an unacceptable risk of being helplessly stranded on the mountain. If an emergency arose, they would be in no position to call for help. I could appreciate Prem's frustration at the vacuum caused by the seven sherpas returning to the Base Camp, but we just had to put together another support party to provide him and N.D. a fighting chance. Also, if they made a premature attempt and failed, it would have had serious repercussions on the morale of the second summit team and effect their chances. So I asked Prem to rest for a day at Camp VI and wait for the support party to reach him.

The same day, Young Tenzing and Gyablo, brought up a ferry from Camp IV and with a little inducement agreed to stay on and make a try at carrying to Camp VII. Then I requested Norbu, one of the second summit party, to do two

134

stages in a day and reach Camp VI in time to join this carry. I was extremely reluctant to strain him like this, thereby possibly endangering the second party's chances for the summit, but he was fit enough to have managed both the jobs. Dorje was already at Camp VII and so now we had managed to muster four people to support Prem and N.D. to the last camp. I would naturally have preferred to have a stronger support party but there was no choice. However, even with these four in position I felt much more confident, particularly since I knew that some equipment, including the tent and five oxygen bottles had already been dumped midway to Camp VII by Prem on May 28. I was now ready to take the chance.

During our wireless transmission that evening, I strongly urged Prem to carry Camp VII as high as possible. Then the wireless set at Camp VI sprung a defect. We could not hear Prem, though he could hear us. Later on we discovered that a wire near the mouthpiece had cracked due to the extremely low temperature. We desperately wanted to know if Prem required anything else from Camp V, which could be sent up with the support party the next day but we just could not hear him. Surjit then thought of a novel variation of the guessing game.

"Hello Prem, do you need anything to be sent up with the support party tomorrow? If your answer is 'yes', just press the pressure switch twice."

We heard two distinct crackles. Now we knew that he wanted something. But what? The guessing game went on.

"Is it anything to do with food?" Surjit enquired.

There was silence at the other end.

"Is it anything to do with climbing equipment?"

Again there was silence.

Surjit then wanted to confirm if Prem was getting our messages. "Please press your switch twice if you got my last message."

We clearly heard twice the crackle of the pressure switch. The guessing game continued. We reeled out a list of over fifty items without getting any positive response. Then Surjit asked, "Has it anything to do with photography?" Prem at once buzzed twice. After a few more questions we knew he wanted some more colour films. "Do you need anything else?" Prem again buzzed twice. And the Kanchenjunga Quiz went on for another half-hour until I asked Surjit to inquire if it were a spanner for the oxygen adapter that Prem wanted. Back came two buzzers. Very reluctantly we asked him if he still wanted anything more and thanked our lucky stars when the wireless set remained silent.

On May 29, the support party started up. I kept my fingers crossed hoping no one would fall sick. We had no means of providing any additional support and only after they had started off did I gradually relax; I could now do little to affect the final outcome of the climb. I still felt they had a chance provided they could take the last camp high enough, and the weather held.

On May 30, the two summiteers and the support party left Camp VI for Camp VII at 7 a.m. The knife-edge arete presented little difficulty, and even though it was roped, most of them hardly used it and slogged through to the Col, where they sank 6 to 8 inches in the fresh snow; and then climbing the face without much effort they reached the dump. So far they had been carrying relatively light loads, but now they had also to take up the stuff that had earlier been dumped there. Heavily laden, their progress slowed down. They would climb a few steps and rest, then start climbing again, only to stop breathless after a few more steps. At this stage they were not yet using oxygen.

Slowly they crossed a snow-field and started towards a ring contour which could be seen from Camp I. Tashi Dorje was beginning to feel exhausted and could climb no more. Putting all he had into it, he tried a few more steps but had to give up; he could not go further. He had done extremely well considering that he had suffered at lower altitudes earlier. Prem and Norbu went back to him and added his load on to theirs. But carrying such loads hampered their progress and Camp VII could not be placed as high as I wanted. Their performance was also affected since they were climbing without oxygen but using oxygen would have meant carrying impossibly heavy loads. Camp VII was pitched at 26,250 feet (7,990 metres), just before the point where the main summit ridge began, and in line with the highest point seen from Camp I. The support party dumped their loads, wished the summiteers all success and started their return journey.

Prem and N.D. had a tough time putting up their small Swiss tent in the strong winds. It was the first time that they were facing the unhampered blast of the westerlies. And this was the lull period prior to the monsoons! The on-coming monsoon winds neutralize the westerlies to a great extent, providing a brief calm before the storm. I wonder if it is at all possible to climb this ridge during normal wind conditions.

Prem and N.D. selected a big rock and pitched their tent on its western flank. Even inside the tent, the strong winds made it extremely difficult for them to light their stove and melt snow for some liquids. We had sent up some roast chicken but they just could not get any solids down their throats. After drinking some juices, they got into their sleeping bags and tried to sleep as best as they could. All through the night, the wind lashed at their tent and tore holes through it. It was a very uncomfortable night for them. Prem hoped they would have better weather on the morrow and could hear N.D. mumbling indistinct prayers to his gods. During the night, they used oxygen at the rate of one litre per minute.

They were up at 4 a.m. and had to go out of the tent to get ready as the tent was too small to move about in, and was also now torn at many places. N.D. tried to light the butane gas stove to melt some snow but their match sticks would not light as these had got damped in spite of their polythene wraps. Finally at 5. a.m. Prem decided to skip breakfast and get on with the climb. Those who have been up at such heights would realize what it means to climb in a dehydrated state. They also did not switch on their wireless set, for they thought that people at lower camps would be asleep. In fact, everyone at lower camps was not only wide awake but also eagerly glued to the wireless set for some news from Camp VII.

While readying their oxygen sets, Prem discovered that one of the regulators was leaking. This was a serious problem. We had earlier tested these regulators again and again, but possibly a washer had come off. Luckily, they were carrying a spare regulator. For the climb ahead, Prem regulated the oxygen flow to a rate of two litres per minute and then they were off.

They first faced a long snow slope. Right from the start, N.D. began falling behind. He felt completely exhausted and could barely drag on for a few steps at a time before sitting down to rest. "I can't go on," he said helplessly to Prem after some time. Prem on the other hand felt very fit and so it struck him at once that perhaps some problem in the supply of oxygen was causing N.D.'s exhaustion. He checked N.D.'s set, and sure enough found that he had not been getting sufficient life-giving oxygen. After he had adjusted the regulator, N.D. immediately felt stronger. Prem asked N.D. to take the lead and set his own pace so as not to get exhausted. Prem writes in his diary, "At first we were barely crawling up but soon N.D. started gaining strength and in a short while he had completely overcome his lethargy." They climbed on for a while through soft snow till they reached a flat tract where they rested and replaced their half-empty bottles with completely filled ones. These half-empty bottles they left at this place for use on the return journey, and climbed on, each having divested one of his two cylinders. At the rate they were using oxygen, the cylinders had sufficient supply for about 9 hours of climbing.

They were now on the western flank of the North Ridge. To their right they could see the West Ridge approaching and culminating at the summit. Finding the going on the North Ridge difficult due to the strong wind, they thought they might find easier ground on the West Ridge. They started a diagonal traverse towards the West Ridge, but soon found it tougher, as they kept sinking knee-deep into the snow on a very steep slope. They quickly retraced their steps to the original route on the North Ridge. This was a wise decision for even if they had got to the crest of the West Ridge, they would have come across severe difficulties. In 1945 too, the British had opted for the South-West Face instead of the West Ridge.

Back again on the North Ridge, they climbed a snowy slope and reached a bare rocky pitch, completely eroded by the westerly winds. However, the gradient of the slope was not very steep and they made steady progress. At 12.30 p.m. they reached the base of a whale-like rock feature. At this point they paused to study the situation. The summit still seemed far away and they considered their position. If they went on, perhaps they would never be able to come back alive. But on the other hand, if they were to return now, three months of hard labour of 60 men, the heavy hazards faced and a life sacrificed, would all be wasted. Wisely they opted to continue for some more time. A little later, they reached the top of the whale-like ridge and the summit dome of Kanchenjunga lay straight

FROM: AKE

TO: INDARMY

PERSONAL FOR THE CHIEF OF ARMY STAFF FROM LEADER (.) YOUR BOYS HAVE
DONE IT (.) MAJ PREM CHAND AND NAIK NIMA DORJE SHERPA GOT TO THE TOP
AT 1454 HOURS (.) .... (.) REGARDS (.)

Prem Chand and N.D. went straight into their sleeping bags. It was now over
24 hours since they had had any liquid to drink but at the moment they had no
strength left even to light the stove. The tent had torn some more since morning
and offered little protection from the wind. Snow kept piling on to their almost
unprotected sleeping bags inside the tattered tent, and the gale kept lashing at
them. But they lay completely exhausted, oblivious to everything around them.

Next day they got up late and started downwards. Later Prem said that the
summit day had been nothing compared to the ordeal of their descent from Camp
VII to Camp VI. It was the hardest day of his life. They had no strength left,
and every step was a living pain. N.D. had gone snow-blind, his eyes were red and
swollen. He kept blinking in an effort to clear his blurred vision. Prem was worried
about getting N.D. across the knife-edge arete. He himself was in no condition to
help him. So he left N.D. and tried to make to Camp VI as fast as he could, with
the idea of sending some help from there. But N.D. too did not like to stay put.
Slowly he kept following Prem's tracks with swollen, painful eyes. The moment
he opened them even a little, the agony got worse, so he would see the route through
the corners of his eye for a moment, then close his eyes and take a few steps. When
help reached him, he was already on the arete. Back at Camp VI, he also complained
of cold feet and later the doctor discovered that he had also got a touch of frost-
bite. But both of them recovered before they reached civilization.

To say the least, Prem and N.D.'s herculean effort is unmatched in the annals
of Himalayan mountaineering. No mountain above 28,000 feet has ever been
climbed from a last camp nearly 2,000 feet below the summit—and that too with
virgin trail ahead. Lord Hunt had said, "There is no doubt that those who climb
Kanchenjunga first will achieve the greatest feat of mountaineering." Prem and
N.D. had not only climbed the most difficult mountain in the world but had
climbed it from its most difficult side.

The Vice Chief of Army Staff, Lt-General O.P. Malhotra (left) flew to Gangtok to receive Colonel Kumar (right) and other members of the Kanchenjunga expedition.

We waited for the debris to settle down and then waded through a labyrinth of 4-foot high ice boulders to get over the dangerous stretch. Once we had crossed that, I finally felt safe.

We reached Lachen on June 9, exactly three months after the first party had left to set up the Base Camp. During our journey to Lachen, the monsoons finally set in and continued throughout our journey to Gangtok. The first night it rained so heavily that half the Northern Sikkim highway was flooded. Three big bridges were washed away. We had come out just in time!

At Lachen, we came to know that Momphali, one of our boys from Ladakh Scouts, had fallen in love with a pretty porter from Lachen and wanted to get married. His friends were against it because of a distance of over 1,000 miles between the villages of the two families. However, I gave him my blessings. One of the members became the boy's guardian and they were engaged.

We were in no mood to walk even a kilometre now. But we then got a flash message that Lt-General O.P. Malhotra, PVSM, Vice Chief of the Army Staff, was coming to meet us at Gangtok on June 16. So we steeled ourselves and marched the 31 miles to Gangtok, in a day and a half for this was a great honour for us.

At all the parties we attended at Gangtok, Momphali was missing. He had arranged to get married at Lachen. But since we had all left the place in a hurry, the ceremony could not be held. He was now lying love-lorn, not interested in anything in Gangtok. I was sorry for the young lover and at once sent him back to Lachen. Sure enough, he found his girl there equally sad. The day after his reaching Lachen they were bound in holy wedlock. The benefits of matrimony started right away. His new bride carried his rucksack on their return journey to Gangtok.

At Gangtok we were accorded an unforgettable welcome by the Governor, Shri B.B. Lal, and the Chief Minister. The people of Gangtok too arranged a grand civic reception. After a week, we returned to Darjeeling and I stayed for three days as a guest of Group-Captain A.K. Chowdhary, the Principal of the Himalayan Mountaineering Institute, a guest in what had once been my own home.

Group-Captain Chowdhary graciously puts me up in my old bedroom. I lie down on the bed and through the window see the majestic Kanchenjunga now swathed in clouds, remembering how often I had felt cheated by destiny at not being able to climb it. Back in the same room, I can vividly recollect the heart-rending ache of having been so close to this mountain for so long yet so far. Now I have kept my tryst with destiny; we have climbed Kanchenjunga. The trail that had kept me going for a good part of my life now lies cold. And another ache, vague and undefinable but almost as powerful, begins to grip me. I feel a great vacuum creeping into me. Kanchenjunga waits for me no more.

APPENDIX I: Members of the Expedition

Col Narinder Kumar, Leader

Aged 44, married. Kumaon Regiment. Born at Rawalpindi in Pakistan. Leader of Trisul (23,360 feet—7,120 metres) expedition in Central Himalayas, 1958. Member, pre-Everest Kabru (24,009 feet—7,318 metres) expedition in Sikkim, 1959. Member, Indian Everest expedition (ht. reached 28,298 feet—8,625 metres), 1960. Leader, successful Neelkanth (21,639 feet —6,595 metres) expedition, 1st ascent, 1961. Leader of successful Nanda Devi (25,645 feet—7,816 metres) expedition, 2nd ascent. Deputy Leader, successful Indian Everest expedition; 9 got to top, 1965. Leader, Indo-Bhutan Chomalhari (23,997 feet —7,314 metres) expedition. Joint Leader, successful Brahma (21,027 feet—6,409 metres) expedition. Climbed Kolahoi, (17,779 feet—5419 metres), Kashmir, 1972. Organised Nan Kun expedition in 1974. Leader, Indo-German Indus Boat expedition, Ladakh, 1975. Leader, Trisul Ski expedition, 1976. Skied down from 23,298 feet (7,101 metres). Principal, Himalayan Mountaineering Institute, 1966–71. Principal, Indian Institute of Skiing and Mountaineering, Gulmarg, 1971–76.

AWARDS: Param Vishist Seva Medal, Padmashree, Ati Vishist Seva Medal, Arjuna Award and Indian Mountaineering Foundation Gold Medal.

Height reached on Kanchenjunga: 25,100 feet—7,650 metres.

Major Prem Chand, Dy Leader

Aged 36, married. Dogra Regiment. Climbed Kolahoi (17,779 feet —5419 metres), 1969. Climbed Harmukh (16,789 feet—5117 metres), 1969. Climbed Chomalhari (23,997 feet—7314 metres), 1970. Climbed Parikan (22,297 feet—6,918 metrès), 1971.

Member, Indo-French Nanda Devi Traverse expedition, 1975. Climbed Nanda Devi East (24,391 feet—7434 metres), 1975. Member, Indo-Japan Nanda Devi Traverse expedition, 1976. Climbed Nanda Devi (25,647 feet—7817 metres).

AWARDS: Kirti Chakra, Vishist Seva Medal, Indian Mountaineering Foundation Gold Medal.

First ascent of Kanchenjunga from North-East Spur.

Major Surinder Surjit Singh, Dy Leader

Aged 34, married. 3 Gorkha Rifles. Climbed Mulkila (21,646 feet —6,598 metres), 1970. Climbed Nun (23,410 feet—7,135 metres), 1971. Climbed Kolahoi (17,779 feet—5419 metres), 1972. Skied down from Trisul (23,360 feet—7,120 metres), 1976.

AWARDS: Sena Medal, COAS Commendation Card.

Height reached on Kanchenjunga: 18,931 feet—5,770 metres.

Major S. Sen

Aged 38, married. Army Medical Corps. Member, Nun (23,410 feet—7,135 metres) expedition, 1971. Member, Gangkar Punsum South (20,791 feet—6,337 metres), 1973. Member, Bunder Punch (20,270 feet—6,178 metres) expedition, 1976.
AWARDS: Vishist Seva Medal.
Height reached on Kanchenjunga: 20,670 feet—6,300 metres.

Major Pushkar Chand

Aged 34, married. Parachute Regiment. Climbed Umba Peak (19,620 feet—5,980 metres), 1974.
Height reached on Kanchenjunga: 25,099 feet—7,650 metres.

Capt Kiran Inder Kumar

Aged 32, married. Parachute Regiment. Climbed Leopargyal 1st ascent (22,277 feet—6,790 metres), 1967. Member, Sasar Kangri expedition, climbed two unnamed peaks (21,500 feet—6,553 metres and 20,500 feet—6,248 metres). Member, Brahma (22,668 feet—6,909 metres) expedition, 1969. Climbed two unnamed peaks in Kishtwar Himalayas, 1970. Member, Indo-Bhutan Kangri expedition. First ascent Kangri III (19351 feet—5898 metres). Leader, Indo-Bhutan expedition, climbed Gangkar Punsam South (21,450 feet—6538 metres), first ascent, 1973. Member, Indo-British Changabang (22,520 feet—6864 metres) expedition, 1974. Member, Indo-American Nanda Devi (25,647 feet—7817 metres) expedition, 1976.
AWARD: Sena Medal.
Height reached on Kanchenjunga: 25,033 feet—7,630 metres

Capt Jai Bahuguna

Aged 28, bachelor. Engineers. Climbed Jogin (19,501 feet—5944 metres).
AWARD: Vishist Seva Medal.

Capt Jude Lawrence Cruz

Aged 28, bachelor. Parachute Regiment. Climbed Frey Peak (18,000 feet—5486 metres).
Height reached on Kanchenjunga: 18,000 feet—5486 metres.

Capt S.A. Cruz

Aged 27, married with one child named Kanchen. Army Medical Corps.
AWARDS: Vishist Seva Medal.
Height reached on Kanchenjunga: 21,980 feet—6,700 metres.

Coy Hav Major Kura Ram (now Naib Subedar)

Aged 36, married. Kumaon Regiment. Climbed Kolahoi (17,779 feet—5419 metres) in 1968. Harmukh (16789 feet—5117 metres), 1970.
AWARDS: Sena Medal, COAS Commendation Card.
Height reached on Kanchenjunga: 21,752 feet—6,630 metres.

146

Coy Hav Major Gurcharan Singh (now Naib Subedar)

Aged 34, married. Sikh Regiment. Climbed Kolahoi (17,779 feet—5419 metres), 1968. Climbed Harmukh (16,789 feet—5117 metres), 1969. Skied down from Trisul (23,360 feet—7,120 metres).
AWARD: COAS Commendation Card.
Height reached on Kanchenjunga: 23,720 feet—7,230 metres.

Coy Hav Major Chhering Norbu (now Naib Subedar)

Aged 33, married. Ladakh Scouts. Climbed Umba (19,620 feet—5,980 metres), 1974. Climbed Sickle Moon (21,677 feet—6607 metres), 1st ascent.
AWARDS: Ati Vishist Seva Medal, Sena Medal, Vishist Seva Medal.
Height reached on Kanchenjunga: 26,230 feet—7,995 metres.

Coy Hav Major Nirmal Singh (now Naib Subedar)

Aged 33, married. Sikh Regiment. Climbed Brahma II (approx. 20,000 feet—6096 metres), 1975. Member, Indo-American Nanda Devi expedition, 1976. Climbed Harmukh, 1969 and Kolahoi (17,779 feet—5419 metres), 1968.
AWARD: Sena Medal
Height reached on Kanchenjunga: 2,3720 feet—7,230 metres.

Naik Nima Dorje Sherpa (now Havildar)

Aged 30, married. 1/3rd Gorkha Rifles. Pre-Everest expedition, 1964. Climbed Raunti, 1967. Climbed Bander Punch (20,270 feet—6178 metres), 1971. Climbed Kamet (25,443 feet—7755 metres), 1973. Climbed Sickle Moon 1st ascent 1975. Climbed Trisul (23,360 feet—7120 metres), 1976.
AWARDS: Kiriti Chakra, Sena Medal.
1st Ascent of Kanchenjunga from the North-East Spur.

Hav Kushal Singh (now Naib Subedar)

Aged 36, Parachute Regiment. Member, Trisul (23,360 feet—7120 metres) expedition, 1973.
AWARD: Vishist Seva Medal.
Height reached on Kanchenjunga: 25,033 feet—7,630 metres.

Hav Jawahar Singh

Aged 30, married. Parachute Regiment. Member, Parachute Himachal Expedition, 1976. Sickle Moon (21,677 feet—6607 metres) expedition, 1975.
Height reached on Kanchenjunga: 20,670 feet—6,300 metres.

Hav Sukhvinder Singh

Aged 31, married. Sikh Regiment. Was member of successful Sickle Moon (21,677 feet—6607 metres) expedition.
AWARD: Shaurya Chakra (Posthumous).
Height reached on Kanchenjunga: 19,488 feet—5,940 metres.
Died on 12 April, 1977 while coming down from Camp II.

Naik Phunchok Angchuk

Aged 30, bachelor. Ladakh Scouts. Climbed Chukal Chumatang (23,000 feet—7,010 metres).
Climbed Tsati Kangin (22,000 feet—6,705 metres), 1976 (Ladakh).
Height reached on Kanchenjunga: 25,038 feet—7,630 metres.

Naik Tashi Dorje

Aged 32, married. Ladakh Scouts. Climbed Bobra Valley Peak (22,000 feet—6,705 metres), 1976.
AWARD: Vishist Seva Medal.
Height reached on Kanchenjunga: 25,919 feet—7,900 metres.

The Support Party of Ladakh Scouts

For the first time boys from Ladakh Scouts (a regiment of the Indian Army) were used on a big expedition like Kanchenjunga in a support role and their performance was astonishing.

Names	Camp reached
1. Nk Gonchak Sonam, VSM	VI (7,630 metres)
2. Sep Rigzin Namgyal, VSM	V (7,230 metres)
3. Nk Cherring Mutup	IV (6,300 metres)
4. Sep Cherring Angchok	IV (6,300 metres)
5. Sep Cherring Tundup	IV (6,300 metres)
6. Sep Stenzon Nurbu	IV (6,300 metres)
7. Sep Chewang Nurbu	IV (6,300 metres)
8. Sep Tundup Tashi	I (5,720 metres)
9. Sep Cherring Nurbu	IV (6,300 metres)

SHERPAS

Our sherpas formed the back-bone of the expedition and without their help we could not have been successful. Apart from sherpas from Nepal and Darjeeling, we also had a group of high-altitude porters from Manali, largely belonging to the Lahul and Spiti area of Himachal Pradesh. I am happy to state that they lived upto the high standards normally associated with sherpas.

148

Name of sherpas	Camp reached

Sherpas from Nepal

1. Ila Tashi, Sirdar (Khunde)	VI (7,630 metres)
2. Ang Pema, Cook (Khunde)	I (5,720 metres)
3. Tenzing Young (Namche)	VII (7,995 metres)
4. Ang Nima (Phorche)	VI (7,630 metres)
5. Mingma Gyalzen (Phorche)	V (7,230 metres)
6. Lhakpa Gyalb (Phorche)	VII (7,995 metres)
7. Pemba Tsering II (Khumjung)	II (5,940 metres)
8. Pasang Gyalzen (Phorche)	IV (6,300 metres)
9. Nima Dorjee (Phakdingma)	VI (7,630 metres)
10. Ang Jangbo (Pangboche)	V (7,230 metres)
11. Lhakpa Dorjee (Khunde)	V (7,230 metres)
12. Nima Dorjee (Pangboche)	I (5,720 metres)
13. Gyalzen Sherpa (Taktar)	VI (7,630 metres)
14. Pasang Tenzing (Khunde)	VI (7,630 metres)
15. Lhakpa Tenzing (Khumjung)	IV (6,300 metres)

Sherpas From Darjeeling

1. Gyalzen Mitchen, Sirdar	Advance Base Camp (5,100 metres)
2. Sonam Tenzing	II (5,940 metres)
3. Mingma Tenzing	VI (7,630 metres)
4. Karma Sherpa	V (7,230 metres)
5. Chhunje Sherpa (Cook)	Advance Base Camp (5,100 metres)

High Altitude Porters from Manali

1. Cherring Namgyal	VI (7,630 metres)
2. Dharam Chand	VI (7,630 metres)
3. Gupt Ram	V (7,230 metres)
4. Lubdu Ram	V (7,230 metres)
5. Sonam Wangyal	V (7,230 metres)
6. Sonam Paljaur	IV (6,300 metres)

APPENDIX II: Glossary
of Mountaineering Terms

ACCLIMATISATION: Physical adjustment to the rarefied atmosphere of high altitudes and the physiological tolerance of these conditions.

ALP: A mountain pasture.

AMPHITHEATRE: A cirque of rock containing a number of routes, or possible routes.

ARETE: A ridge of rock or ice.

AVALANCHE: A sudden fall of rock, snow and ice either singly or collectively.

BELAY: An anchor point on a climb from which protection can be afforded. Also used as a verb indicting the fastening of oneself to such a point, and giving protection to companions.

CAIRN: A pile of stones to indicate a summit, any other height or route-marker.

CHIMNEY: A vertical fissure in rock or ice in which the body can be jammed for climbing purpose.

COL: A pass.

CORNICE: Overhanging snow projecting over the edge of a ridge, formed by wind.

COULOIR: A french word for gully, ravine or wide cleft.

CRAMPONS: A framework of metal spikes strapped to climbing boots to give purchase on ice and hard snow.

CREVASSE: A vertical fissure in a glacier that can be very wide and deep. Caused by the movement of glaciers over uneven ground or bends.

DESCENDER: A mechanical device used for abseiling or coming down a fixed rope.

FIRN/NEVE: Snow which is in the process of turning into ice and becoming part of the upper reaches of a glacier.

FIXED ROPES: Ropes used as anchors and hand rails to facilitate the transport of loads and for rapid movement.

GENDARME: A pinnacle or rock tower forming an obstacle on a mountain ridge.

GLACIER: A slowly moving river of ice.

HARNESS: An attachment of webbing worn round the chest or waist or. both, for anchoring a climber to the rope.

ICE-AXE: An axe used for cutting steps in snow and ice and maintaining balance on steep slopes.

ICE FALL: When a glacier falls over a steep step it forms a confusion of ice cracked with crevasses and seracs. Such an area is called an Ice Fall.

JUMAR: A metal device to slide along a fixed rope while climbing.

KARABINER: A metal with a clip on one side which is closed by the action of a spring. It is attached to the eye ring of a piton and holds the rope which runs through it.

MORAINE: Accumulation of stones, and debris carried down by a glacier.

PITCH: A section of a climb between two stances or belay points.

PITON: A metal peg that is used as anchor in ice or rock with karabiners, ropes and tapes.

SADDLE: A depression in a ridge between two summits.

SCREE: A mass of broken stones, varying in size, on the side of a mountain or in a gully.

SNOW-BLINDNESS: Inflammation of the conjuctive, a painful condition due to excessive exposure to ultra violet rays reflected from snow and ice.

SNOWLINE: The point at which snow starts on a mountain.

TRAVERSE: Moving across a face or slope, or a horizontal climb.

WINDSLAB: A hard crust of snow plastered onto older snow by wind.

APPENDIX III : Acknowledgement
For Help to the Expedition

FIRMS

1. Fabino Shoe Ltd, U.S.A.
2. Mohan Meakin Breweries Ltd,
3. Gillanders Arbuthnot & Co Ltd, New Delhi
4. Hindustan Vacuum Glass Ltd, New Delhi
5. West Coast Manufacturers & Traders, New Delhi
6. The General Fibre Dealers Ltd, (Tea Division), Calcutta
7. State Bank of Bikaner and Jaipur
8. Engineers India Ltd, New Delhi
9. Fertilizer Corporation of India, New Delhi
10. Delhi Cloth Mills, New Delhi
11. Canteen Stores Department (India) Bombay
12. Ajudhia Textile Mills Ltd, Delhi
13. Ideal Engineers Hyderabad Ltd, Hyderabad
14. Tractor India Ltd, New Delhi
15. The Punjab and Sind Bank Ltd, New Delhi
16. Philips India Ltd, New Delhi
17. Water and Power Development Consultancy Service (India) Ltd, New Delhi
18. Steel Authority of India Ltd, New Delhi
19. Hindustan Photo Film Mfg Co Ltd, Madras
20. Bharat Electronics Ltd, Jalahali
21. Escorts Ltd, New Delhi
22. Bokaro Steel Ltd, Bokaro
23. Metallurgical Engineering Consultants India Ltd, Ranchi
24. Bhilai Ispat Ltd, Bhilai
25. Indian Petrochemicals Corporation Ltd, Baroda
26. Rajpal & Sons, New Delhi
27. Hind Pocket Books Pvt Ltd, New Delhi
28. Forgings Pvt Ltd, Faridabad
29. Satnam Nanita & Associates, Chandigarh
30. Surinder Construction Co, Chandigarh
31. National Co-operative Development Corporation, New Delhi
32. Vikas Publishing House Pvt Ltd, New Delhi
33. Canara Bank, Janpath, New Delhi
34. The New Bank of India, New Delhi
35. Vijaya Bank Ltd, New Delhi
36. Agfa-Gevaert India Ltd, New Delhi
37. Prashad Exporters, New Delhi
38. Mohinder Nath and Co, New Delhi
39. Rajasthan Spinning and Weaving Mills Ltd, New Delhi
40. Belpahar Refractories Ltd, Calcutta
41. Advertising Associates (P) Ltd, Madras
42. Supreme Mountaineering Equipment Industries, New Delhi
43. Allied Publishers Pvt Ltd, New Delhi
44. Indian Oxygen Co Ltd, Calcutta
45. Phoebus Stoves, Austria
46. NELCO, Delhi

152

ORGANISATIONS

1. Ministry of Tourism and Civil Aviation, New Delhi
2. Government of Sikkim
3. Indian Embassy, Kathmandu
4. Indian Embassy, Bonn
5. Indian Embassy, Washington
6. Indian Embassy, London
7. Indian Airlines
8. Indian Mountaineering Foundation
9. Controller General Imports and Exports
10. Department of Research and Development, Ministry of Defence, New Delhi
11. All India Radio, New Delhi
12. Defence Food Laboratories, Mysore
13. Assam Rifles
14. Director-General, Ordnance Factories
15. Himalayan Mountaineering Institute, Darjeeling
16. Meteorological Department, Government of India
17. Sherpa Climbers Association

INDIVIDUALS

1. General T.N. Raina, MVC
2. Air Chief Marshal H. Moolgavkar, PVSM, MVC
3. Lt-General O.P. Malhotra, PVSM
4. Lt-General A.M. Vohra, PVSM
5. Lt-General J.F.R. Jacob, PVSM
6. Lt-General J.S. Nakai, PVSM
7. Lt-General H.C. Rai, PVSM
8. Lt-General E.A. Vas, PVSM
9. Lt-General Kundan Singh, PVSM
10. Lt-General A.M. Mathur, PVSM
11. Lt-General R.D. Hira, PVSM, MVC
12. Lt-General R.P. Sapra
13. Lt-General W.A.G. Pinto, PVSM
14. Lt-General P.V. Ramachandran, PVSM (Retd)
15. Lt-General M.M.L. Chabbra, PVSM (Retd)
16. Lt-General S.P. Malhotra, PVSM
17. Air Marshal J. Zaheer, AVSM, PVSM, Deputy Chief Air Staff
18. Major-General S.C. Sinha
19. Major-General N.C.S. Menon
20. Major-General A.K. Bhattacharya
21. Major-General I.M. Vohra, MVC
22. Brigadier Inder Sethi (Retd)
23. Brigadier P.N. Kathpalia
24. Brigadier Teg Behadur Kapur, AVSM
25. Brigadier T.S. Verma
26. Brigadier M.N. Rawat
27. Brigadier C. Venugopal, MVC
28. Brigadier V.S. Sharma
29. Lt-Colonel Bhisham Kumar, VSM
30. Lt-Colonel J.C. Joshi
31. Lt-Colonel C.S. Nugyal
32. Lt-Colonel D.N. Tankha, AVSM
33. Major Satish Mahindroo
34. Major P.K. Vasudeva
35. Major Bhupinder Singh
36. Major N.R. Naidu
37. Captain Jaspal Singh
38. Captain K.K. Marwah
39. Captain A. Kohli
40. Havildar Ghanshyam Prasad
41. Naik Clerk Shiv Narain Sharma, ASC
42. Shri H.C. Sarin
43. Shri S.S. Gill
44. Shri N.B. Menon
45. Colonel J.O.M. Roberts
46. Group-Captain A.J.S. Grewal
47. Shri Tenzing Norgay
48. Shri N.K. Banerjee
49. Cdr Joginder Singh
50. Shri Nawang Phinjo
51. Shri Dorjee Lhatoo
52. Shri Ang Temha
53. Dr Vijay Raghwan

Index